A Framework For CRM In Bu Using Artificial Int

by
Kaur, Jaspreet

Abstract

Today customers are highly exposed to the essential amount of information related to products and services like never before. This leads to an enormous amount of diversity leading to consumer's demand, thus becoming a challenge for the retailers to cater right products and services as per customer's preferences. Customer reviews, opinions and shared experiences related to a product turns to be an effective source of information about customer's preferences that can be utilized by recommender systems. To recommend products to the users, buying list of users, viewer's list and purchase count of the products are considered as main fundamental attributes for conducting the analysis of the products purchased and viewed. In this, a hybrid recommendation model that combines machine learning, collaborative filtering and data analytic is proposed. The recommendation algorithm begins to acquire cluster of similar users. Further, Similar shopping basket of customers is prepared with User-item matrix and purchase count of the products. The data set is then clustered as per the requirements to form train-test data. The Experimental Results shows low error i.e. lower root mean square and has high precision and high response time in comparison to Popularity based (Baseline) recommendation model. Owing to today's modern transformation from visiting retail stores to online purchases, predicting consumer behavior in e-commerce is becoming extremely valuable. This will improve customer loyalty and purchases, leading to increased transaction rates and a competitive advantage, by encouraging a more personalized customer experience. This article evaluates machine learning models to predict purchases. Customer Relationship Management systems have been used to allow businesses to attract new customers, develop a long-term relationship with them and improve the retention of customers for greater profitability. CRM systems use machine-learning models to evaluate personal and behavioral data of customers to give company a competitive edge by increasing the retention rate of customers. These models can predict customer's purchases, and their reasons. Predictions are used in the development of targeted marketing plans and service offerings. This section focuses to develop a framework by applying machine learning techniques to predict the purchases by the customers on e-commerce platform. Through clickstream and additional customer data, frameworks for predicting customer behavior can indeed be developed. Predicting potential consumer behavior generates pertinent information for sales and marketing teams to strategically focus on different resources. Such information facilitates inventory planning at the warehouse and at the point of sale, as well as strategic decisions during production processes can be planned accordingly. Next, this research provides insight into the performance differences of the models on sequential clickstream and static customer data by performing a data analysis and training the models separately on the various datasets. Deep Belief network along with auto encoders and Adam optimizer is performed to validate the data and predict the likelihood of purchase and customer conversion probability. Chatbot is now-a-day widely popular and catching pace as a computer communication tool. Like humans, some programmes interact intelligently. This software type is called a Chatbot. In current scenario, users are quickly turning to social media for quick customer service; however, most of these complaints were in vain and are not dealt in a timely manner or have not even been answered at all. To solve this issue, a new conversational system has been developed to automatically produce answers to user requests on social media. This paper looks at developing and implementing a Chatbot system.

ACKNOWLEDGEMENT

My first and foremost sincere thanks to **Dr Harsh Sadawarti (Vice Chancellor, CT University, Ludhiana)**, for providing me this opportunity to carry out this thesis work.

The Constant guidance and encouragement received from department of research committee members for their great help in carrying out the present work and is acknowledged with reverential thanks.

I would like to express a deep sense of gratitude and thanks profusely to my thesis Supervisor **Dr Harsh Sadawarti, (Professor, Department of Computer Science Engineering, School of Engineering & Technology).** Without the wise counsel and able guidance, it would have been impossible to complete the thesis in this manner.

I express gratitude to other faculty members of Computer Science Engineering Department, CT University, Ludhiana for their intellectual support throughout the course of this work.

Finally, I am indebted to all whosoever have contributed in this thesis work and friendly stay at CT University.

(JASPREET KAUR)

TABLE OF CONTENTS

CONTENTS			PAGES
	Candidate's Declaration		i
	Abstract		ii
	Acknowledgement		iv
	Table of Contents		v
	List of Figures		ix
	List of Tables		xi
	Nomenclature		xii
Chapter 1	Introduction		1-21
	1.1	Introduction	1
	1.2	Background	1
	1.3	Customer Relationship Management	1
	1.3.1	Features of CRM	2
	1.3.2	Importance of CRM	4
	1.3.3	Reasons for adopting CRM	5
	1.4	Relationship between CRM and Artificial Intelligence	6
	1.4.1	Advantages of AI integration with CRM	9
	1.5	Artificial Intelligence(AI)	10
	1.5.1	Classification of AI	11
	1.5.2	Applications of AI	13
	1.5.3	Impact of AI on Businesses	15
	1.6	Predictive Analysis	17
	1.6.1	Applications of Predictive Analytics	18

	1.6.2	Predictive Analytics in CRM	20
Chapter 2		**Literature Review**	**22-40**
	2.1	Predictive Analysis	22
	2.2	CRM	28
	2.3	Data Mining	33
	2.4	Recommender Systems(RS)	39
	2.5	Similarity Finding	40
Chapter 3		**Present Work**	**41-44**
	3.1	Gap Analysis	41
	3.2	Problem Formulation	42
	3.2.1	Objectives	44
Chapter 4		**Proposed Work for Recommending Products**	**45-59**
	4.1	Data Collection	45
	4.2	Purchase Recommendation	46
	4.3	Similarity Finding(Cosine Similarity)	46
	4.4	Experimental Setup and performance Analysis for Recommending Products	49
	4.4.1	Data pre-processing	50
	4.4.2	Training and Testing Data	54
	4.4.3	Recommending Products	54
	4.5	Results and Discussion	55
Chapter 5		**Proposed Work for Predicting Purchases**	**60-67**
	5.1	Data Collection	60
	5.2	A Random Forest Classifier	61
	5.3	Experimental Set u for Predicting Purchase	63

5.3.1	Data Pre-Processing	63
5.3.2	Attribute Selection	63
5.3.3	Predictive Modeling	63
5.4	Results	64
Chapter 6	**Proposed Work for Predicting online behavior of users**	**68-85**
6.1	Data Description	69
6.2	Classifiers	70
6.2.1	Ensemble Method	70
6.2.1a	Bagging with Random Forest Model	71
6.2.1b	Boosting	72
6.3	Deep Neural Network	72
6.3.1	Deep Belief Network	72
6.3.2	Auto Encoders	74
6.4	Experimental Setup for Online Behavior of Customers	76
6.4.1	Data Preprocessing	76
6.4.2	Non-Negative Matrix Approximation	78
6.4.3	Regularization	79
6.4.4	Optimization	80
6.4.4a	Adam Optimizer	81
6.5	Results	82
Chapter 7	**Developing a Virtual Assistant in respond to Business Services**	**86-93**
7.1	Introduction	86
7.2	Implementation Process	86
7.3	Results	93

Chapter 8	**Conclusion & Future Scope**	95
References		97

LIST OF FIGURES

Figure No	Figure Description	Page No.
1.1	CRM Features	4
1.2	AI based Solution to CRM	7
1.3	Classification of Artificial Intelligence	11
1.4	Percentage of AI start-ups in different sectors of business	16
1.5	Types of Predictive Modeling	18
4.1	Proposed Model for Product recommendation	45
4.2	Similarity concept by cosine degree	47
4.3	Collaborative Filtering Technique	48
4.4	Snapshot for Single Item	51
4.5	Snapshot for merged four weekly items	51
4.6	Customer who purchased the products	52
4.7	Customers who viewed the products	52
4.8	Input table prepared for modeling	53
4.9	User-Item matrix	53
4.10	Train & Test Sets	54
4.11	Comparison between Proposed Algorithm and Popularity based (baseline) Algorithm	56
4.12a	RMSE of Proposed algorithm and Popularity based (baseline) algorithm	57
4.12b	Precision- Recall summary of proposed algorithm & Popularity based (baseline) Algorithm	58
4.13	Response Time of Proposed algorithm and Popularity based (Baseline)	59

5.1	Proposed model for Purchase Prediction	60
5.2	Random Forest Prediction Model	62
5.3	Attribute Selection	63
5.4	Decision tree formed from Random data samples	64
5.5	Data Visualization after attribute selection	65
5.6	Random Forest Model results	66
5.7	Logistic Regression Results	66
5.8	Random Forest ROC Curve	66
5.9	Logistic Regression ROC curve	67
6.1	Layout of the Autoencoder	75
6.2	Dropout value of Regularization	80
6.3	Denoising AutoEncoder with Epochs and Loss	80
6.4	Adam optimizer Result	82
6.5	AUC Curve for different Classifiers	83
6.6	Dispersion of pageview occurrences for a subset of the data	85
6.7	AUC for conversion probabilities and purchase likelihood	85
7.1	Logic Implementation in Chatbot to respond to random answers	90
7.2	Dictionary of intro, greet and end intents	91
7.3	Running server and configuring the system	92
7.4	GUI based Chatbot interaction	93
7.5	Response from the Chatbot	94

LIST OF TABLES

Table No	Table Description	Page No.
1.1	Studies dealing with CRM and AI	8
4.1	The first schema corresponds to Category database which contains only two attributes, while second schema corresponds to events database which consist of three different types of events namely; add to cart, view and bought while third and fourth schema corresponds to item properties	52
5.1	Description of all Dataset files	60
6.1	Parameters for Clickstream	70
6.2	Dataset framed for testing models	78
6.3	Metaparameters considered for training the dataset	84

NOMENCLATURE

ABBREVIATIONS	MEANING
CRM	Customer Relationship Management
AI	Artificial Intelligence
PA	Predictive Analytics
ASI	Artificial Super Intelligence
ANI	Artificial Narrow Intelligence
AGI	Artificial General Intelligence
SVM	Support Vector Machines
DLN	Deep Learning Networks
RS	Recommender System
AAL	Ambient Assisted Living
ADL	Activities of Daily Living
ODHM	Online Daily Habit Modeling
RTI	Radio Tomographic Imaging
NLP	Natural Language Processing
MO	Multiple overimputation
CMM	Customer Mindset metrics
SOM	Self-organizing Maps
CLV	Customer Lifetime Value
TF	Term Frequency
IDF	Inverse Document Frequency
RMSE	Root Mean Square Error
DT	Decision Tree

MDI	Mean Decrease in impurity
ROC	Receiver operating Characteristic
AUC	Area under ROC curve
KPI	Key Performance Indicator
RF	Random Forest
DNN	Deep Neural Network
BP	Back Propagation
DBN	Deep Belief Network
RBM	Restricted Boltzmann Machinery
NMA	Non-negative Matrix Approximation
ReLU	Rectified Linear Unit
NLTK	Natural Language Processing Toolkit

CHAPTER 1: INTRODUCTION

1.1 INTRODUCTION

This chapter begins with background of Customer Relationship Management (CRM) and further leading to CRM integration with Artificial Intelligence (AI). This section provides detailed discussion about Artificial intelligence, Predictive analytics (PA) and the research problem formulated there from, along with the research motivation in order to complete this thesis.

1.2 BACKGROUND

Customer Relationship management or CRM originated early in 1970's (Juneja 2019). CRM software hasn't always been a robust and standalone application that most of the businesses rely on today. The evolution of CRM has been divided into number of stages. It has developed gradually from a variety of other business programs beginning from pen-paper, Rolodex software, database marketing and contact management software to today's social and mobile CRM automated software over the past three- four decades (History and Evolution of CRM Software 2017; CRM Switch 2020).

1.3 CUSTOMER RELATIONSHIP MANAGEMENT

In this ever rising competing environment, companies need to focus on maintaining positive relationship with their customer. Most of the Companies make exhaustive use of technologies to capture and store customer information. This trend has also spread its wings in relationship marketing, leading to new forms of customer relationship management (CRM).

CRM as a word states, is defined as the process of integrated data driven solutions for maintaining a relationship with their consumers and help improve the business. It is a hostile mechanism of consumer identification, attraction, differentiation and retention. It also helps in building customer value by integrating organisation's entire supply chain at every stage, either by lowered costs or increased benefits. It helps keep revenue, customer support, promotions, field operations and other customer functions perfectly coordinated. It is because of CRM, organizations recognise their customers, tailor their needs and service, understand their demands and offer products as per their needs that can serve as a significant asset to them.

1.3.1 Components of CRM

i. Customer

ii. Relationship

iii. Management

1.3.2 Features of CRM

CRM is considered as a strategy for achieving excellence in businesses by administrating its customers and vendors in an effective manner (Juneja 2019). The top CRM features include (Juneja 2019; Bonanno 2019 and Adair 2018) and are also depicted with the help of a figure1.1:

- **Contact management** – It is considered as main key factor in customer satisfaction and an important element of CRM. This feature allows segmenting the contacts into groups and organizing them in a better way. With this CRM capability, it helps to collect important data of the customers and helps in planning better marketing strategies after a new product is launched.

- **Customer Needs** – To maintain a long term relationship, it is essential to know the needs of the customer to serve them effectively. To know and prioritize a customer, it becomes important to interview them about their likes and dislikes.

- **Customer Response** – It is defined as the response given by the organization to their customer's queries or request. It plays a crucial role in gaining the customer's confidence and maintaining a long term relationship with them. All it takes to understand the customer's queries with patience and providing a satisfactory solution to it.

- **Customer Satisfaction** – In today's competitive environment, customer satisfaction is one the biggest differentiating factor considered in business strategies and an

important performance factor. It is defined as how the customer needs and responses are collaborated and delivered to excel the customer satisfaction.
- **Lead management** – This feature allows a business to find their best customers based on their demographics features.
- **Product Support** – CRM software helps effectively collect the information about various products and services offered to the customers. This information helps manage the customer experience as it helps in organizing the information about what, when and how and with what the client is dissatisfied and how as that issue addressed.
- **Data Reporting** – This is the most prominent feature of CRM software. It helps to create flexible and realistic customer database. Without this feature, it is difficult to find customer behavior, trends or the actions needed to be taken to improve their relationship with the customers.
- **Sales Analytics** – Considered as one of the most important component of CRM. It collects all the data from different sources like social media, forums, website, polls, etc and then analyzes it. Further, it helps to create better campaigns by analyzing the past data campaigns.
- **Mobile CRM** – With emerging technologies, everything these days is available at ease to the users and to benefit the business. With this feature, it takes CRM on remote device using mobile CRM apps and programs and one can receive alert messages about their campaigns on a mobile device.

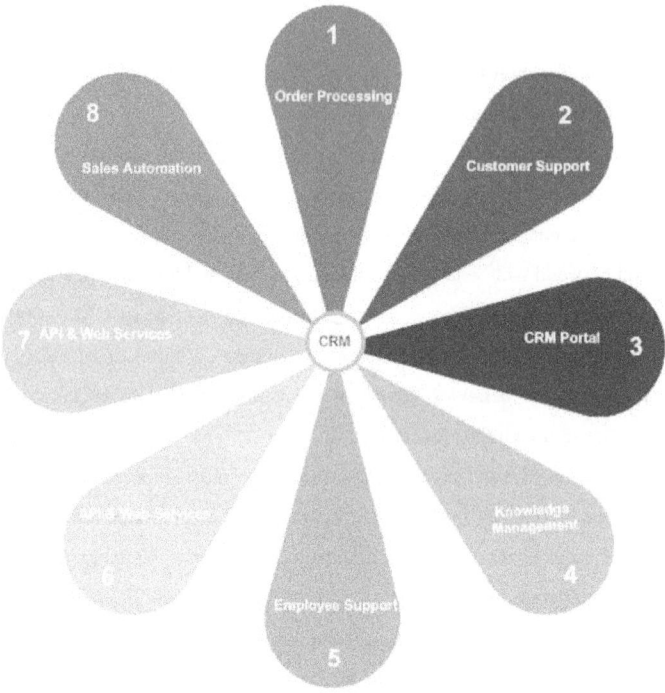

Figure 1.1: CRM features

1.3.3 Importance of CRM

CRM is must for all those business who desires to take customer satisfaction to a higher level (Salesforce). For this to be achieved, it is important to deploy proper CRM tool, which helps to track and manage all the interactions and communications your representative have with the customers(Baker 2016). There are several benefits of using CRM in any business (Salesforce; Baker 2016):

- Enhanced Communication
- Improved Customer service
- Automations of tasks
- Organized Customer data

- Segmentation of customers
- Creating Sales Reports
- Sales Performance analytics
- Improved Analytical data reporting
- Make administrative tasks efficient

1.3.4 Reasons for adopting CRM

As the Competition to lure customers is increasing day by day and is becoming intense, it is necessary to build lasting and lucrative relationships with their valuable customers. Companies realized from an economic point of view that keeping an existing client is less expensive than looking for a new one. It has been observed that a long term customer is more valuable than a single deal customer. As described in the Theory of Pareto, it postulates that two thirds of the customers of business earn 80 percent of its revenue. In company, marketing a product or service to new customers needs average 7 to 10 physical calls in person and about 2 to 3 calls for a potential regular client (Bhatia 2008). Repeating business from an existing customer is easier than acquiring a new customer. On average, an increase of 4-5 percent in maintaining current customers results in an increase in profitability of 20 percent or more. CRM helps in recognizing the value of customers and it aims at building lasting and profitable relationships with them (History and Evolution of CRM Software 2017). Companies who prioritize the relationships with the customer tend to create a strong connection with them, thereby, increasing the customer lifetime value, and to promote customer loyalty. There are several ways by which even a small scale company can get advantage from, is by, encouraging customers to visit their website, communicate through different platforms on social media such as Instagram, Twitter, Facebook, etc and by reading or commenting on blog posts, etc. The main purpose of the companies is to develop trust and captivate customers and reduce the customer churn.

One of the best methods for building a strong relationship with the customer is focusing on an emotion. A combination of various processes and set of some useful systems in CRM helps in building a good business plan and this approach to business results in increased profits of a business by influencing customer behaviour. This furthermore helps to boost customer acquisition, customer satisfaction and customer retention, loyalty and profitability. Most businesses are unsure about their customer interaction, programme's efficiency, effective data storage, meeting customer needs, etc. As an immense amount of data is produced by interaction with users, it becomes a great challenge for organizations. Rivas 2020, stated to overcome these challenges and transform them into new significant opportunity, CRM is integrated with Artificial Intelligence (AI).

1.4 RELATIONSHIP BETWEEN CRM AND ARTIFICIAL INTELLIGENCE

With the advancement in technologies, machines have the potential to coordinate their conventional tasks that go beyond humans in their traditional functions of organizing, accumulating and disseminating data as per user's requirement. As a result, this advancement has resulted in evolution of Artificial Intelligence (AI). The chunks of data companies possess that of customers and the numbers of resources customers are utilizing to communicate with businesses have significantly outgrown in the past decade. Artificial intelligence technology holds the assurance for raising high economic benefits, enhancing customer and client communications.

The word "Intelligence" in this context refers to the competence of machines to acquire, comprehend, determine and deliver exactly as that of humans. AI assists businesses automate customer outreach and make optimum usage of data (Rivas 2020). It provides with the surpassing solutions and weed out the natural error "Human Error" which, however, is inexcusable by customers. Due to accelerating competition among established brands and start-ups; loyalty, customer satisfaction, customer care has become priorities. A team of qualified and competent employees is required to ensure high customer retention and to execute various tasks as below:

- Searching new potential customers
- Conversion of visitors to customers
- Selling the product
- Retaining customers
- Generating Economic benefits

AI has emerged as an analytical solution to the frequent challenges faced by employees as depicted in the Figure 1.2.

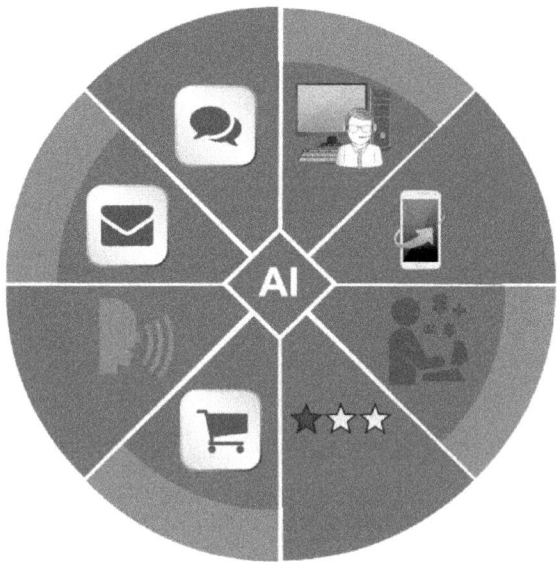

Figure 1.2: AI based Solution to CRM

AI can help boost productivity by virtue of allowing the personnel to intensify the things which can help organizations or firms raise their standard. They can concentrate better on issues which involve human interaction, such as building stronger connections with customers. It will help to remove the stress of menial tasks, which are always unavoidable and must be thoroughly done. Artificial intelligence provides the assistance in managing various issues such as disorganized data, calculation errors, incorrect names or numbers, and thus, preventing the dealings to call off with a challenging customers. Each company handles tremendous amounts of data and inbound information can be handled more easily and faster thereby, utilizing the true potential of employees in a better way and by not unleashing it in solving the menial tasks.

Table 1.1: Studies dealing with CRM and AI

Reference	Title of paper	Objectives
Mekkamol et al. (2013)	Modelling e-CRM for community Tourism in Upper Northeastern Thailand.	To develop e-CRM model for community tourism in Upper North-eastern Thailand
Charoensukmongkol & Sasatanun (2017).	Social media use for CRM and Business performance Satisfaction: The moderating Roles of social skills and social Media sales intensity.	To study the association between intensity of the customer relation management with social media usage and Performance satisfaction of Businesses.
Alami et al. (2017)	Artificial cognition for social Human Robot cognitive interaction: An implementation	To discuss the collaborative-skills working implementation and original architecture for Human-robot interactions
Goyal et al. (2017).	Deep learning for detecting Inappropriate technique Content in text.	Proposed a novel deep learning for identifying inappropriate Content.
Luo (2016)	AI- based methodology of integrating affective design, engineering And products marketing for defining Design specifications.	To propose a method for integrating engineering and marketing of new designs at An Early stages of new products
Bressgott et al (2019)	How artificial intelligence will change	To discuss how marketing

| | the future of marketing and customer Behaviour. | strategies will change in Future and proposed Multi-dimensional Framework for understanding How AI will change the Behaviour of the customers In future. |

1.4.1 Advantages of AI integration with CRM

- **More Efficient Data management** – In CRM, all Social Media data can be centralized for the AI to view and provide real value to the goals of the organization (Rivas 2020).
- **Improved Consumer Comprehension**– Like humans, the primary motive of AI is to constantly learn. An AI would be more accurate in evaluating and studying consumer trends critically, which would eventually boost CRM (Mills 2018).
- **Tailored Plan for Sales** - Through Automated data entry and predicting customer behavior, companies can provide material of real interest to their customers and can establish strategies that can increase the engagement level of customers.
- **The Perfect Assistant-** Implementing Artificial intelligence in CRM helps to create more effective marketing campaigns, by sending and handling messages without any direct feedback. It requires quite a lot of time away from the companies to distinguish the client on its interests, spending patterns and history. Using AI powered CRM, however, can handle the data effectively and easily. By sending automated alerts based on quickly evaluated data, the platform makes recommendations on how and when to call, thus increasing the productivity and efficiency of its employees.(Rivas 2020)

- **Increased Customer Satisfaction** - By using a user-friendly marketing strategy targeted at the right moment and in the right context, businesses can help their consumers build positive feelings about their brand.

1.5 ARTIFICIAL INTELLIGENCE(AI)

AI is defined as the human intelligence inculcated in machines and programmed to think and behave like human beings (Frankenfield 2020). AI is often referred to as an interdisciplinary science that deals with building smart machines that performs tasks just like humans. Virtually, every area of tech industry either Machine learning and deep learning innovations are producing an exemplary transition (In 2016). Artificial Intelligence, powered by advancements in computing power, is the next great wave of innovation. It can store enormous amounts of data in the cloud at a minimum cost. It is considered as a most disruptive and powerful shift in technology in comparison to the previous years.

There are several terms used to represent AI: machine learning, deep learning, natural language processing, predictive analytics, etc. All these terminologies represent a platform on which our future will be based and system will be smart enough to determine our interactions and data to anticipate one's need, to help understand what is required, to remind forgotten tasks. AI helps us to integrate our personal, social and professional life into one experience that moves flawlessly with us from one place to another. Our phones are one of the examples which helps us to experience this to most of the extent. In future, AI will be interpolated in all digital products.

As customers, we are already using AI without even realizing it. Facebook news feeds, Google assistant to search queries, amazon product recommendations, self driving cars, etc, are all applications of AI which predicts with great accuracy. These applications are custom-tailored for us via machine learning algorithms. All these applications have trained consumer's mind in such a way that they have become accumulated with them and have started expecting more from businesses (CRM 2016).

1.5.1 Classification of AI

AI and AI-enabled machines can act or feel like humans imitating just like human minds. Therefore, these machines can be classified (Bali and Nayak 2020) as depicted in Figure 1.3

- Reactive machine systems for example: Deep Blue is one such machine which defeated Kasparov at Chess in 1977.
- Limited memory machine systems
- Mind theory systems
- Self-aware AI

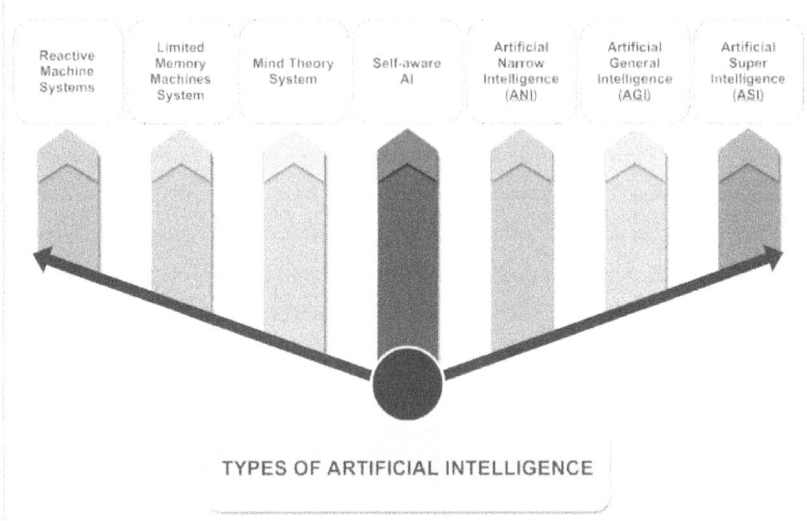

Figure 1.3: Classification of Artificial Intelligence

a. **Reactive machines**: Recognized as a most basic types of Artificial intelligence. These AI machines do not have the capability of storing memory or any previous experience for performing future actions. They lay emphasis on the current scenario and react in a best possible way. These machines are purely designed for some specific tasks and can't be implemented in any other situation. They behave exactly in a similar way every time they encounter the same situation and cannot participate interactively in the world. Examples of these systems are: Google's Alpha-Go for defeating Top human Go experts and IBM's Deep Blue super computer for playing chess (Point 2015 and Hintze 2016).

b. **Limited Memory Machines**: These Type-II machines are capable of storing limited data or past experiences for a shorter duration. This stored data can be used for a limited time only. They have the ability to learn from the historic data and to frame their own decisions. Almost all the applications existing today fall under this category. Large volumes of training data have been used to train all Existing AI systems, including deep learning technique. This data is stored in their memory as a reference model for solving future problems. Examples of these systems are: Self-driving cars, Virtual assistant and chatbots, etc are all driven by limited memory AI (Point 2015; Hintze 2016).

c. **Theory of Mind:** This is category III type considered as work in progress next level of AI systems, which the practitioners or researchers are now engaged. This type still exists as a work in progress. Theory of mind level AI will be able to understand and interpret the things they'll interact with by comprehending the emotions, beliefs, needs, thought process and interacting just like humans. A lot of efforts are required by the researchers to develop such machines. With AI already being the rising industry and to achieve Theory of mind level, it requires the AI to indulge in other areas as well to better understand the human mind and their needs. To better understand human mind, AI machines have to perceive humans as an entity whose mind is formed by various factors, leading to understand the Humans. (Point 2015; Joshi 2019).

d. **Self-Aware AI:** Considered as a future and the final step of Artificial intelligence. These futuristic machines will be super intelligent with their own self-awareness, consciousness and sentiments. Being an extension of the Type III or Theory of mind AI, will help build systems that will be able to form representations about themselves, smarter than human mind. Developing self-aware systems can boost the progress and once they are capable of having the idea of self-preservation, they can easily outmaneuver the intellect of any human being. The alternate classification which is more prominently used in technology these days is the taxonomy into Artificial Super Intelligence (ASI), Artificial Narrow Intelligence (ANI) and Artificial General Intelligence (AGI) (Point 2015; Joshi 2019)

1.5.2 Applications of AI

AI as discussed is the simulation of human intelligence and imitating human mind by the machines with great efficiency. It is already advancing and transforming the world economically, socially and politically. Some of the applications of Artificial intelligence are described below (Pannu 2015; Bhosale et al. 2020):

a. Artificial Intelligence in Healthcare

Healthcare sectors are deploying Artificial intelligence to make better decisions and diagnosis at a much faster rate than humans. AI technology helps imitate human intelligence into ICT that helps in assisting both the doctors and patients. Mycin was the expert system developed in 1970, for identifying the cause of infections and recommending antidotes to treat them. Another system developed was Pathfinder, which used Bayesian networks for diagnosing Lymph nodes. AI has worked as a game-changer in healthcare industry and has provided the doctors with the leverage of reducing their schedules, free up their time, reduce cost, etc. It has helped the laboratory agents for analyzing medical information, conducting various experiments and for making better decision via various tools. AI has also been effective in medical imaging for computer-aided identification of tumours and has assisted in the diagnosis of different types of cancer and ischemic heart disease.

a. Artificial Intelligence in Robots

Implementing AI in robots helps reduce the workload on humans in one way or the other. It helps enables the response at the time of disaster for any dangerous situations occurring at the time of emergency. It will help decrease the traffic accidents and deaths. AI in Robots will help in taking care of aged people and allow them with longer independence.

b. Artificial Intelligence in Education

In education sector, Artificial intelligence has played a surprising role, may it be teaching or learning process. It has changed the scenario of education. Using AI, helps in better analyzing the students, their performance. It makes it possible for the teachers to provide automated grading to different types of question format, may it be multiple choice or fill-in-the-blank types. There are many AI based tutoring programs which help students have a basic understanding of mathematics, writing, etc. AI makes it easier for the students to learn from anywhere, anytime in the world. AI powered educational programs are helping students to learn and understand basic skills. With the increase in the demand of AI based programs, students will be offered with wider range of programs (Borge 2016)

c. Artificial Intelligence in business

The implementation of Artificial Intelligence in industry has been widespread. Several types or levels of AI are implemented in business. Machine learning algorithms are deployed into CRM to serve their customers in a better way. Chatbots have just been consolidated into sites and e-organizations to offer quick support to clients. Robotization of employment positions has additionally become an argument among scholastics and IT consultancies. In every one of these parts where man-made reasoning permitted frameworks exceed expectations. Computer based intelligence gives exact and proficient information.

d. Artificial Intelligence in Travel and navigation

In transportation enterprises, AI is emerging as one of the significant key for this business. For the formation of travel plans — artificial intelligence is consistently helps individuals in their everyday life. With the help of AI- travel assistance, people are able to reserve trips and learn travel tips. Chatbots is likewise utilized by travel industry for providing services regarding notifications to the clients, details about booking, etc.

Google Maps AI is one such example related to travel industry which helps user in recognizing street information, for identifying fastest route for cars, buses, bikes and by walk too (Pannu 2015; Bhosale et al. 2020).

1.5.3 Impact of AI on businesses

In general, AI advancement is the cornerstone of the updated execution of all other advancements and leading to Industry 4.0 evolution. There are adequate pieces of evidence available in the writing that shows that the AI technology provides new openings that can lead to exceptional market change depicted in figure 1.4 and therefore affecting the overall economic system. At the commercial level, a few of the benefits of AI are:

- Speedy unveiling of big data trends,
- Rapid visualization and analysis
- Progressed product plan
- Business expansion
- Improved efficiency etc.

It is expected that these benefits will bring new service levels, raised profit and market growth, enhanced quality and price structures.

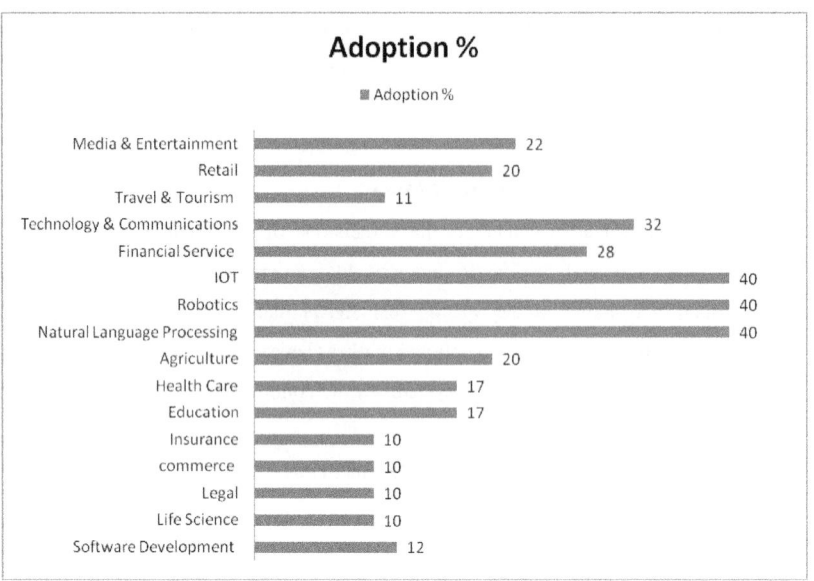

Figure 1.4: Percentage of start-ups with AI in various market sectors (Soni et al. 2018; Low 2018)

In today's scenario, every real-world applications are backed by an intelligent agent. To communicate with the environment, this agent follows a repeated pattern of sense-think-and-act. It analyses the input data to understand correlations, extracting features, for detecting similarities, and discovering good depiction at various levels. Prior to this, the inaccessibility of knowledge and efficient equipment had impeded AI's advancement. However over the last few years, the accessibility of low-cost and low-power sensors has resulted in the generation of a huge amount of data. For exploring input data, AI or machine learning instruments such as support vector machines (SVM), Bayesian algorithms, deep learning networks (DLN), decision trees and ensemble configurations are needed. Over the last few years, DLN has become the most successful algorithm (Soni et al. 2018). Various Business intelligence applications are developed using different algorithms to detect patterns, trends and for creating insights using company's database or external inputs. Over the next ten years, business intelligence applications are projected to be one of the fastest growing fields of AI technology. HANA is one of the examples of use business intelligence. The cloud systems of SAP help businesses handle their database (Geisel 2018).

1.6 PREDICTIVE ANALYSIS

Have you ever thought about how Facebook knows who you can include in your "Friend" list or how well-timed purchase proposals are communicated by Amazon? These are some of the important applications involving the use of Predictive Analytics (PA). This specific type of analysis creates quantifiable and sometimes thrilling market outcomes that can be seen all around us. Predictive analytics incorporates current information from multiple sources. It can build models that can be used to improve future outcomes using a blend of art and science as stated by Dhimas 2012. Predictive analytics is often seen as the next stage to expand the growth of data analytics and to hone decision-making to boost performance of the business in advance (Lepenioti et al. 2020). In order to improve decision-making, predictive analytics can generate useful information for the management of supply chain companies. This would be useful for the estimation of demand, identification of faults, maximization of hardware value, preventive maintenance, optimization of marketing strategies, consumer keeping and industry aftermarket service association. Predictive analytic does not aim in telling what is going to happen in future. It helps to predict what will happen in the future with an acceptable degree of precision and consistency. It helps businesses find good opportunities for them and possible risks. It also helps to better understand their customers, their goods and their business as discussed by Mohanty and Ranjana (2019).

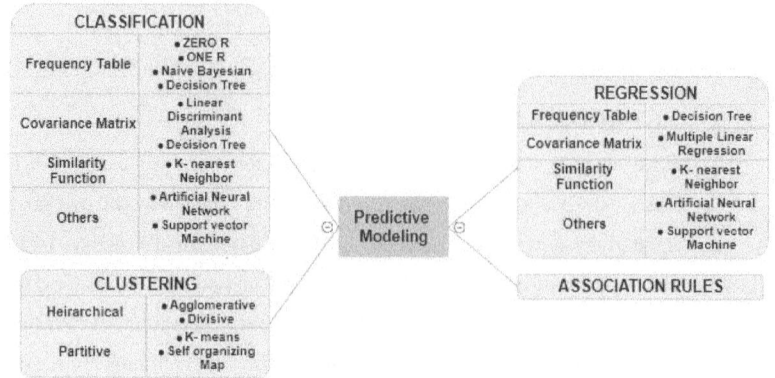

Figure 1.5: Types of Predictive Modeling

1.6.1 Applications of predictive analytics

Predictive model can be applied in different sectors depending on its application (Mahmoud 2017).

a. In Education Sector

Predictive analytics have been used widely used in education sector for different purposes with the help of various models and tools. The benefit of using predictive analytics in education sector will help the institutions to enhance their student's results and achievements and at the same time help increase the retention rate of the students too. This application can also be beneficial in predicting the student's performance in their specific courses and to find those students who have chances of low performance and high chances of failing in the exams. Various algorithms used were association rule, decision tree, etc.

b. In Manufacturing Sector

Implementation of predictive analytics in manufacturing field has been widely increased. In this field, PA is able to predict the power consumption in metal cutting industry with the help of big data infrastructure. PA is highly valuable in this field. By anticipating the changes in manufacturing system states, it contributes to production improvement corresponding to cost, quantity, quality and sustainability. It can lead to improve productivity gains, if efficiency in design and production is increased.

c. In Social Media

With the extensive increase in the usage of social media, it is difficult to handle the data that has been generated by the users via traditional means. The data so generated has tremendous amount of information which can further be useful to various government and private business organizations. It involves lot of effort in analyzing that data and extracting the right amount of information useful to the organizations. Social media in a way disseminates the information way before the traditional media do it. Therefore extracting the different patterns, graphs, statistics help the organizations with different feedbacks valuable to them and extract the right amount of information required for their business (Mukonyezi 2015).

d. In Transportation

In this sector, predictive analytics helps in predicting the arrival and departing time of buses and train via smart public transportation decision support system. Clustering model was used for detecting the patterns of bus performance along with the irregular operations (Mahmoud 2017).

e. In Business Sector

Implementing predictive analytics in business have been useful in understanding the customer's behavior, products, partners and their market. It helps in identifying the hidden patterns, potential risks and opportunities for a company. It helps in predicting the future aspects by analyzing their historical data. The foremost important aspect in business is to retain the customers; with these organizations will be able to understand the priority of customers, their demands and the satisfaction level of them (Mohanty and Ranjana 2019).

f. In Health Care Sector

Today's healthcare organizations confront expanding weight to realize way better care coordination and improve patient's t care results. To achieve this, organizations are turning to predictive analytics. This area of insights deals with the utilization of machine learning algorithms, anticipating the probability of future results based on past information. Predictive analytics can be utilized in healthcare to "identify pain points all through the stages of intake and care to enhance patient's experience and healthcare delivery.

1.6.2 Predictive Analytics in CRM

The consequence of predictive analytics in CRM is a growing trend. It is one such technique that enables businesses to explore and learn consumer habits, attract and retain consumers, and also maximize customer value. Thus it promotes the making of CRM decisions and helps build Marketing strategy in a customer-centered economy. Management of customer relationships is known as one of the most significant management activities in businesses. CRM is defined as a combination of systems and methods that help to create long-term and successful strategic relationships with customers. Successful CRM techniques are therefore based primarily on customer data.

Predictive analytics have, for many years, been used enormously in the telecommunications and banking sectors to recognize consumer behavior and profitability. Predictive analytics methods have been rapidly applied in the last few years to other businesses engaged in B2C transactions. Big data theory and the ability to generate usable knowledge from existing databases are main determinants of the predictive analytics implementation. Thus, more companies hope to be affiliated with suppliers of PA.

By analyzing transactional and historical market data, predictive models are used to recognize the challenges. The predictive models raise awareness of the connections between distinctive data bits and identification of the root factors of consumer behavior as well as possible market insufficiencies to make informed decisions about customer experiences. Hence, Predictive analysis is also impressively distinct from conventional business intelligence methods. In order to delineate past patterns and organizational outcomes based on chronicled data, traditional BI methods are useful, while predictive analytics can forecast, inform decisions and anticipate future consumer and business developments. IT tools expedite the implementation of predictive analytics in CRM. One of the CRM principles emphasizes IT as an important method for companies to nurture deeper customer relationships and promotes customer data analysis to provide detailed insights into customer behaviour in order for CRM to become the basic infrastructure. A robust CRM architecture contains two key components that are both operational CRM and analytical CRM. For the most part, the focus of the CRM systems implemented till date is on enhancing CRM's operational perspectives, such as innovations to gain customer inquiries and solve challenges to maximise customer loyalty and satisfaction. Operational CRM gathers customer information through a number of product lines, including mail, sales, call centre, call management system, fax and website. The information is stored in a client-centric database in this framework that is available to all users in an enterprise to communicate with their clients. Analytical CRM in any case focuses mainly on consumer data mining and analysis. A combination of analytical tool is adopted in the analytical CRM method to evaluate customer information stored in databases and render their profiles and segmentations, and to detect associated patterns in customer behaviours and predict the degree of customer satisfaction. These analytical methods help to assess the value of customer's benefit and also to classify the customer who is likely to churn. Analytical CRM and the use of data-based analytical techniques are thus becoming more important and widespread for customer analysis, customer experiences, and benefit management. Organizations that are empowered with analytical CRM software will cultivate better procedures and allow more proficient use of their resources. In supporting the analytical CRM systems, numerous advances are recognised, among which "CRM portals," data warehouses," "predictive and analytical engines," "sequential trends," "clustering," "classification "and" customer value assessment" are addressed by various researchers. In the analytical CRM system, predictive analytics (PA) tools is a prominent ways to analyse consumer data. As a result of this study, consumers are more easily segmented and managers are able to make informed decisions about their consumer relationships while delivering customer-based products and services. (Lepenioti et al. 2020).

CHAPTER 2: LITERATURE REVIEW

Artificial intelligence these days is playing a vital role in business and transforming the economy. The idea of artificial intelligence is not only restricted to workflows but the artificial intelligence as revolutionized the customer experiences in business communication as well. Most top business companies are now using AI which has in turn increased the demand for the best AI-powered CRM. CRM infused-AI is still in its initial days. Therefore this section is split into five parts namely Predictive Analytics (PA), Customer Relationship Management (CRM), Data mining, Recommender System (RS) and Similarity Finding. The former section discusses the role of Artificial intelligence and predictive analytics in various domain including CRM and the published papers of AI and PA whereas second section explains the published work in the field of CRM, third section describes the use of data mining technique in CRM along with other fields, fourth section describes the recommender system deployed in various domains and last section discusses about the similarity finding techniques.

2.1 PREDICTIVE ANALYSIS

Schlogl. S et al(2019) examined the applicability of AI tools in different technologies and also studied the human attitude towards these technologies. Around 19 interviews were conducted to know the usage of AI tools in different European companies. Consequent results states that utilization of AI and its technologies is still at the starting point by various companies. The reason behind the lack of usage of these technologies is the missing information and the lack of relevant skills. These companies are merely using it for the effectiveness of their internal processes or for the management of Customer relationships for determining their social media tasks. These companies are merely using it for the efficiency of their internal processes or for Customer relationship management for data mining their social media tasks. With those who managed to get their foot into the AI application field had to face a dominance of in-house AI implementation. This was caused due to lack of trust on third party service providers. They further emphasized that this issue seems to be of particular significance in view of recent amendments in European data privacy regulations. Implementation of AI tools was a social hurdle challenge that needs to be overcome. In the prevalent fear of job loss, it was stated that there is lack of employee acceptance which needs to be taken care of. This has evolved with respect to how this type of technology may boost the quality of work without replacing vital aspects of the human workforce.

Kumar and Ranjan et. al. (2019) wrote an article to examine the effect of AI on companies. Their main objective was to investigate the role of artificial intelligence (AI) in the development of a personalized marketing engagement strategy. They concentrated on designing, engaging, and providing clients with customized offerings. This article demonstrates that consumers are ready for a new journey in which AI can encourage real-time learning with endless choices and information that can help executives maximize customer loyalty over time with the help of personalized predictions. It also provided forecasts about the AI-driven environment for managers on branding and customer management activities in both developed and developing countries.

Chagas et al. (2018) analyzed literature studies using techniques of machine learning to enhance or automate CRM tasks. They have included an overview of the practical consequences for each dimension and aspect of the CRM. They also provide insights into current trends in existing CRM tool and provide an outline for potential studies to develop their analytical and automated services and aspects relevant to it. The applications of machine learning and artificial intelligence in the field of CRM were also explored and the study found that the most commonly used techniques in machine learning in relation to CRM are logistic regression, neural network, decision tree and SVM. It also mentioned that the two most reviewed and researched contexts in CRM literature are customer attraction and retention. The analysis of this paper will help researchers and practitioners understand how ML can improve CRM operations effectively and provide insights into the less oriented dimension of CRM and how to strengthen them.

Syam and Sharma (2018) discussed that how Fourth industrial Revolution i.e Artificial Intelligence, machine learning, digitization, Robotics etc influence the decision making and shift the paradigm from humans to machines. They focused on the impact of AI and machine learning on personal sales and Sales management.

Huang (2018) introduced how AI is reshaping service by performing different tasks. They developed a theory of AI job replacement addressing their impact. Service tasks include four intelligences – Analytical, mechanical, empathetic and intuitive. They laid out a way for the organizations to decide between machines and humans to accomplish their tasks. They believed that AI job replacement takes place essentially at the project level rather than at the job level and for activities involving lower (easier) knowledge.. Gradually with time, the progression of AI task replacement can be seen from lower to higher intelligences. Their theory implied that AI will take over more analytical tasks thus; making analytical skills less important and making "softer" intuitive and empathetic skills more important for service employees. Ultimately, AI will be able to perform even the empathetic and intuitive tasks as well, enabling creative ways of integrating human–machine for offering service.

The growing relationship between public relations and AI is discussed by Galloway and Swiatek (2018). To improve the capabilities of a company or agency public relations departments, they are increasingly opting Artificial Intelligence (AI). They outlined the diversity of practitioners in public relations and the variety of AI usage. Based on the developments and their consequences for their employers, customers and practitioners, they addressed various primary AI roles. They believed that much focus was put earlier on the use of AI for task automation, but with regard to the technical, economic and societal consequences of AI, public relations needs critical attention. Practitioners need to gain an understanding of the possible applications of AI, which will provide advice and information.

First, Pereira et al (2018) developed a temporal preference model capable of detecting the preference event transition of the users. These days, the study of these temporal user expectations dynamics has become extremely important for personalization tasks in the realms of information retrieval and recommendation systems.. Secondly, to investigate the evolution of social relationships, they used temporal network principles and proposed methods for detecting changes in the network structure based on node centrality. Finally, for an association between preference change events and node centrality change events, they used Twitter and jam Social music datasets. Their results concluded that there exists a strong correlation between both change events mainly carrying out social interactions by means of temporal network.

Tan et. al. (2018) discusses the challenges of controlling elderly behaviour in the context of ambient assisted living (AAL). Under the paradigm of online daily habit modelling (ODHM), they have used emergent representation for daily living activities (ADLs) along with position-based stigmergy. In order to perform the tasks of recognizing ADLs, they combined with neural convolution networks (CNNs). To break interruptions, they proposed a new paradigm of activity summarization. Promoted and used radio tomographic imaging (RTI) and position-based AAL systems to facilitate the required position-based stigmergy and to comprehend ADLs respectively. In addition, CNN's emerging data aggregation and deep learning together allow the recognition of ADLs at a fine-grained level, contributing to ODHM's performance improvement. Experimental findings indicate the feasibility of the method proposed.

Balonin et al. (2018) laid emphasis on an important role of matrices in digital signal processing, mathematical natural sciences and systems of artificial intelligence all together. They concentrated on the study of the world of matrices that runs intensively across the globe and provides reliably useful and unpredictable outcomes. They presented some of these findings and paid particular attention to Hadamard matrices and some of their improvements and extensions, which are important in turn for the development of artificial intelligence systems and the study of genetic code. They said Training courses or experts with new knowledge of matrices and their functional implementations should be continually updated.

Bradlow et al. (2017) examined the probability of big data in retailing sector. They focussed on five major data dimensions – time, products location, channel and most importantly data pertaining to customers. The statistical concerns that further centered on the use of Bayesian analytical techniques (borrowing, updating, augmentation and hierarchical modeling of data), predictive analysis using big data, and some field studies, all in a retail sense, were addressed. They also highlighted the privacy and ethical concerns emerging from the retail sector's use of big data.

A novel deep learning-based technique for automated identification and screening of inappropriate language was introduced by Yenala et al. (2017) to express, analyze and share their views or opinions on internet discourse online. To enhance the quality of conversations with users or virtual agents, this issue is considered most significant. Two application scenarios(a) User conversations in messengers and (b) Query completion recommendations in search engines focused on solving this problem. They suggested a new "Convolutionary Bi-directional LSTM(C-BiLSTM)" deep learning architecture, which is the combination of Convolution Neural Networks (CNN) and Bi-directional LSTMs (BLSTM) to classify inappropriate queries. For filtering inappropriate conversations, they used LSTM and Bi-directional LSTMs (BLSTM) sequential models. The model so proposed is trained end-end as single model not relying on hand crafted features only and is affective in capturing both local features and global semantics.

Sohrabi et al. (2017) examined the information systems (IS) publications to design a predictive solution to cluster and assess the knowledge domain and to group similar documents together using text clustering methods. This predictive learning approach helped researchers to identify the most suitable articles for their researches via an automated system. These articles were obtained from scopus repository. They utilized K-means clustering algorithm, other different classification algorithms and analytical methods such as Natural Language Processing(NLP), text normalization to evaluate each cluster and the findings were based on the frequency of their words and key phrases. This approach to prediction allows many researchers to recognize the usability for future study of many papers.

Roll & Wylie (2016) discussed that the field of artificial intelligence (AIED) has undergone remarkable developments in past 25 years. They examined 47 papers from 3 years (1994, 2004 and 2014) in the history of Journal of AIED to find the typical scenarios and important focuses that occupy the field of AIED. These findings were used to suggest two parallel research strands that need to take place in order to influence education in the next 25 years: Firstly an evolutionary mechanism that draws on existing classroom activities, instructor collaboration, and technology and domain diversification. Secondly, a transformative process in which we insist on incorporating our technology into the daily lives of students, thus fostering their cultures, traditions, aspirations, and societies.

Kwong et al. (2016) proposed an AI-based methodology based on AI that combines affective design, engineering, and marketing for defining design requirements of new products in this paper. With this step, in the early design phase, the three processes can be considered simultaneously. This approach put more emphasis on developing customer satisfaction and cost models using fuzzy regression, generating functions of product utility using chaos-based fuzzy regression, formulating and solving a multi-objective optimization model using a genetic algorithm of non-dominated sorting-III (NSGA- II). To evaluate the efficiency of the proposed methodology, they conducted a case study for electric iron design.

Redzebra(2016) proposed a robust classifier for purchase prediction. This model forecast purchasing intentions for a large e-commerce website based on user behaviour. To model the prediction, they applied machine learning algorithms, including deep neural networks. This study discussed the two techniques: Two Deep Belief Network and stacked denoising auto-encoders, which achieved significant improvement by extracting features from high-dimensional data and also proved to be helpful in coping with severe class imbalance.

Gupta and pathak (2014) proposed a framework for predicting purchase by online customers with the application of machine learning algorithms. The study focussed on predicting purchase decisions and the revenues benefits based on adaptive or dynamic pricing of a product. Their study was facilitated by statistical and machine learning models along with data mining methods which further utilised different data sources that were gathered from purchase history, web data, visitor attributes and context understanding. They considered customer segment rather than individual buyers for predicting their purchase. This framework was tested on large datasets for en E-commerce firm by selecting an appropriate price range based on Dynamic pricing. Their results determined much better price range appropriate both for customers and an organisation. They also stated that this framework can be applied to any industry working in online mode and can be customised accordingly.

Mirzaei and Iyer (2014) provided a classification framework for predictive analytics (PA) application and Customer Relationship management (CRM) tools and to fulfil the gap between literature review and classification scheme for it. This paper aims to provide a systematic overview of literature published in both academic and practitioner journals between 2003 and 2013 relevant to the application of predictive analytics in CRM. The five CRM dimensions have been identified: customer acquisition, customer attraction, customer retention, customer creation and growth of customer equity. They said that predictive analytics techniques are primarily used to forecast customer attrition in companies and to make informed choices for customer retention. They also suggested that PA techniques are used in the growth of consumer equity to estimate a customer's lifetime value. In the literature discussed so far, less emphasis has been placed on consumer acquisition and customer appeal. They discussed the most prevalent predictive analytics techniques applied are segmentation, Logistics Regression, Markov Chain and decision tree. They identified the multiple regression technique as a better model in comparison to neural network and decision tree in terms of interpretability of the parameters in the literature. As per their review, CHIAD and C5 algorithms were suggested for visual presentation and MATLAB was used for programming among the published articles.

2.2 CRM

Venkatesean et al (2019) offered a solution to individual level predictions of customer profit with a new method called multiple overimputation(MO). In this missing data was treated as an extreme form of measuring error and ascribe the Customer Mindset Metrics (CMMs) for both customers with observed, though with measurement error, along with the missing values, that were then included as predictors in a model of individual customer profits. Their results demonstrated the predictive and economic value of applying MO in the context of CRM models with CMM with the help of a simulation study, empirical application in the pharmaceutical industry, and a customer selection exercise enables firms to predict customer behaviour in terms of sales, retention and profits. They also illustrated a four step procedure to leverage CMM data even when it was just available for certain subsets of customers. Furthermore, they also explained that their MO approach was also applicable to self reported data in general.

Osman and Ghiran (2019) proposed a new method for improving customer's experiences. They emphasized on the new approaches and techniques for generating customer traces from CRMS. And supporting different business processes without having information about the analyzed process. They extracted graphical visualisations with the help of different mining algorithms. Different diagrammatic models were evaluated using different modelling languages such as BPMN, Petri Nets and Casual Nets. They stated that these approaches can be utilised together with Data mining techniques or machine learning techniques to offer best solutions in customer behaviour analysis.

A chapter was written by Venkatesean et al. (2019) to explain how customer engagement is useful for generating value for businesses across the customer lifecycle, including customer acquisition, development, retention, and win-back. Identification of main research in the areas covered by some of the CEV metrics of CLV, CIV, CKV, and CRV has already been included. They focused on determining the promising areas of future research that have enabled researchers and executives to better understand when and how to make better customer service decisions using the various aspects of CEV. The research opportunities were also outlined by including a summary table of questions that had to be taken into account when addressing during each stage of the customer relationship lifecycle. They addressed econometric models built to forecast customer benefit and also claimed that predictive models were inadequate to classify customers with high CRV, CIV or CKV. In addition to model structures, they noted that it is also important to explore the data sources internal and external to an enterprise to recognize the various types of customers. Finally, they said that if businesses can develop and execute customized experiences with different consumer needs and involve their clients, they can succeed in their plan for customer engagement.

Ali and Lee (2018) discussed the sales prediction model for Automotive CRM based on customer interaction. They introduced new machine learning approaches for predicting sales and also discussed its merits, challenges and opportunities in pattern discovering. They also explored a novel idea of computationally learning salesmanship and discussed the success factors for driving industry intuitions for predicting vehicle sale. This developed model helped the users to act as a virtual guide or trainer for the general CRM user population and to keep the salesperson on right track.

Batista et al. (2018) explored the theoretical and managerial implications of effective CRM and simple CRM. They stated importance of organizational responsiveness and how it is used to respond to market changes. They considered the role played by CRM in supporting this process and laid more stress on how organizations approach CRM and embed them. Effective information systems and Staff empowerment features were also considered. An empirical study of financial services firms in Brazil helped to draw an implication stating that improved organizational responsiveness is more efficaciously conducted by CRM approach along with system effectiveness- Staff empowerment rather than simple 'CRM approach'.

Hopkinson et al. (2018) introduced the use of AI to handle customer relationships. They claimed that as recent developments in AI are being applied in this area, CRM will experience vast changes. They addressed the ability for AI to be used in customer relations management.

Bhagat and Muralidharan(2018) presented the model for repeat purchase recommendations. This work has driven positive results both offline and online with the 7% increase in the products click through rate. This experiment was conducted on the amazon.com website based on personalized recommendations. With the successful testing, it has further resulted in the launch of different customer-facing features on different platforms such as Amazon.com website, mobile app and other websites related to Amazon. The Amazon mobile app was launched on different countries like Germany, India. Japan etc.

Goncarovs (2017) presented data analytics as a part of CRM. He explored the integration of CRM with the different characteristics data analytics for sales managers. He analyzed different analytics methods and tools which can be furthered aimed to make continuous improvement for CRM processes.   As the data deluge problem supplanted the data scarcity problem so the Customer Relationship Management (CRM) specialists have much access to huge data on consumer behavior. The main task is effective utilization of these data in CRM processes and selecting the best and appropriate data analytics techniques. Data analytics techniques play an important role in finding the hidden patterns in data. So, Goncarovs conducted a systematic literature to achieve this goal and its results of the review highlighted the most frequently considered CRM processes in the context of data analytics.

Holy.V et al. (2017) proposed a data driven approach for clustering retail products based on customer behaviour using market basket data. They formulated a model as an optimization problem which was further solved by a genetic algorithm. The categorization of retail products helps businesses decision making. They demonstrated their work in simulated data how it behaves in different settings. The main parameter of their algorithm is the number of clusters. This paper demonstrated that their method yields additional information about the structure of the product categorization if more clusters are allowed than the original number of categories.

Arunachalam and kumar(2017) evaluated the performances of different clustering approaches for hunting the profitable customer segments in th UK hospitality industry. They conferred new Insights of novel clustering algorithms application for benefit based market segmentation. The three dimensions on which this paper focused are high dimensionality, ordinal nature of data and outliers. Data was collected from 513 sample points and was further analysed using four clustering approaches: Hierarchical clustering, K-Medoids, Fuzzy Clustering, and Self-Organising Maps (SOM). The findings of this paper suggested that SOM and fuzzy based clustering techniques were more efficient than traditional approaches. Moreover, the case study presented in this paper illustrates how SMEs who are presumably data poor could also generate business value from data mining and analytics application.

Husain (2014) proposed strategies based on Sugar CRM installation. They used data mining techniques to analyze and present recommendations which are useful to various users. An automated approach to business intelligence is followed which can help improve the key performance indicators (KPIs) for businesses using SugarCRM.

Recommendations made to the users are considered as most important outputs that effect KPIs of the business. To have a better understanding of the dynamics of their own business, Data mining are used. In the Industry, they are used for predicting patterns from CRM datasets.

Ruivo et al. (2014) suggested a model which defines the value of integration of Enterprise Resource Planning (ERP) and CRM systems. Resource Based View (RBV) of the firm was used to describe the integrative value and it help to measure the impact on the firm's performance. The model recommended six hypotheses to be tested and analysed with data which was collected from a questionnaire among firms adopted with both ERP and CRM systems in their organization. Partial Least squares (PLS) method was adopted to analyze the data as it was not tested earlier. This model aims to provide the knowledge on how integration between different systems can make a positive affect from IT investments and therefore leading to process integration.

Baecke and Poel(2012) augmented acquisition models with spatial information for improving customer identification prospects. They compare two models such as Autoregressive and hierarchical that incorporates spatial information applied on large datasets in CRM. This study was applied to identify new customers by conducting investigation on 25 brands and products, which were further divided into three categories to improve the predictive performance of customer acquisition models. The results demonstrates that a multilevel model performs well when a discrete spatial variable is used to group customers into mutually exclusive neighbourhoods and also it gives satisfactory results for a large number of durable goods which is significantly better than a frequently used auto logistic model. Further, this application determines interesting observations for marketing decision makers. It indicated that neighbourhood effects can be identified for publicly consumed durable goods. However, it gives worst predictions for consumer packed goods as there is low involvement of consumers and are privately consumed. In other words, for identifying Customers for more exclusive brands, it suggested that incorporating spatial information will not always result in major predictive improvements. For these luxury products, the high spatial interdependence is used in which the spatial variable was represented as a substitute for absent socio-demographic and lifestyle variables. As a result, these neighbourhood variables lose a lot of predictive value on top of a traditional acquisition model that typically is based on such non-transactional variables. This paper clearly indicated that spatial interdependence should not e neglected for certain types of goods as it can help improve a customer acquisition model [64].

Amroush et al. (2008) aims at deciding the best CRM based on their business needs using AI techniques. The assessment model based on AI helped to define the workflows and different needs of the masses who want to purchase the CRM framework. They have listed an RFP-process example that helps choose the best decision-making method to select the optimal solution for their business needs.

2.3 DATA MINING

Zhou et al. (2019) proposed a framework to manage a relationship between banking organisations and their customers. To predict the behaviour of the customers in the real world and to increase the decision making process in identifying the valued customers for their banks, they applied neural network and association rules as two data mining techniques. Their findings indicate that both applied models attain good predicting performances but the neural network technique achieved the best result with accuracy of 97% but taking bit longer time than usual.

Pathan et al(2019) compared market basket analysis using apriori algorithm and market basket analysis without using algorithm. This Comparison was done to create a rule to generate the new knowledge. The comparison focused certain indicators which included concept, the process of creating the rule, and the achieved rule. The comparison results shows that both methods utilized the same concept, the process of creating the rule was different, but the rule itself remained the same.

Carnein and Trautmann (2019) proposed a stream clustering algorithm named "userStream" applicable on customer segmentation. This algorithm was capable of identifying and tracking the custom segments over the time without performing any recalculations. The biggest challenge faced by the authors was the customer segmentation and it relies on the transaction history and data also changes with the time. So it needs to be incorporated into clustering model over and over again to update customers. The proposed model solves this challenge by removing the customer from its cluster whenever a new transaction took place. Then these values were re-inserted into the model as a new observation and the cluster was adjusted accordingly. By carefully selecting the data structure, it removed the recalculation problem of the entire model.

Abdi and Abolmakarem(2018) proposed a Customer Behaviour mining framework in a telecom company y using data mining techniques. This framework predicts the way the customers may act in the future by considering their behavior patterns. They divided their framework in two phases. In the first phase, they used clustering technique to implement the portfolio analysis and dividing the previous customers on the basis of socio-demographic features by using K-means algorithm. Cluster Analysis was conducted on two criteria: no of hours spent on telecom services and number of services selected by the customers of each group. Customers of six groups were identified in three levels of attractiveness as per the customer portfolio analysis. In Second phase, future behaviour of the customers was mined which determined the attractiveness level of the new customers. The framework so developed helped the telecom managers predict their customer's behaviour and develop the appropriate tactics depending on the Customer's cm behaviour.

Manigandan et al. (2018) addressed Business Intelligence (BI), which represents a package that includes algorithms for data mining, data mining products for report development. They also discussed about improving the efficiency of BI. M-Clustering algorithm is used in this process which helps in providing solutions to clusters in two-folds- historical data processing and setting of boundary limits during filtering. Data sets are defined by filtering various attributes and field which further acts as training datasets to get the expected output. Experimental evaluation is carried out in this proposed system with customised algorithms in WEKA tool and efficiency of experimental data is compared with k-means evaluation.

Guo and Qin (2018) analysed the various application fields of data mining techniques for CRM and then explored that how application of data mining applied to Customer churn analysis. They discussed how data mining have shaped CRM and provided a new era, where organisation can gain a competitive advantage, and help in the better management decision. They stated as the market strategy is gradually becoming Customer oriented focussing more on customer satisfaction. Therefore it has become important to understand customers' need which in turn, has become the driving force of most modern business.

Dhamgani et al. (2018) proposed a hybrid soft computing approach for predicting segments of new customers in customer focused companies. This procedure is a combination of clustering algorithm with decision trees classification algorithm for identifying group of customers with high and low values and the new customers with their level. On the basis of their purchase behavior, K-means algorithms were applied to cluster the previous customers of a company based on their value. This cluster so framed was considered as a target variable. For predicting new customer segments and to extract the decision rules based on customer characteristics, classification tree was built. They also proposed hybrid feature selection method to determine the customer's features based on different filtering algorithm and TOPSIS method. The results of the proposed model are set of IF-THEN rules, framed on the basis of customer characteristics and decision tree analysis to help predict insurance companies their potentially profitable leads.

Belarbi et al. (2016) provided a summary of big data analytics on Retail industry. They stated that big data analytics is not only confined to one industry but it can be utilised in another fields too. They portrayed the impact of big data analytics on retail sector and the emerging benefits that are helping to improve marge. They further stated in order to utilise big data, retailers can make use of analytic techniques and technologies to have a better decision making.

Bhandari et al. (2015) proposed an improved apriori algorithm by reducing the number of transactions to be scanned and the time consumed in transactions scanning for specific customer item-sets. This algorithm was proposed taken into consideration the memory space which is reduced when large numbers of transactions were performed on the repositories and the data warehouses. It further explained their concept by stating whenever the m of m-itemset increased the gap between their improvised Apriori and the original Apriori increased from the time it was consumed, and whenever the value of minimum support increased, the gap between their improvised Apriori and the original Apriori decreased from the time it consumed. The time consumption by improvised Apriori algorithm was 67.87% less than the time consumption by the original Apriori, in generating candidate support count. Improvised Apriori algorithm used parallel algorithm and clustering method with the help of which memory space was reduced to be successfully implemented in real time applications especially in library as it gave all the information about the books which were frequently read, thus saving lot of time.

Baharia and Elayidomb (2015) proposed an efficient CRM-data mining framework. They studied two classification models – Neural Network and Naïve Bayes and stated that accuracy of Neural Network is comparatively better than Naïve Bayes. This framework establishes close customer relationships and helps manage the relationship between an organization and a customer. During recent years, Data mining has gained importance in CRM field and classification model is one of the main data mining techniques. To enhance the decision making process for retaining valued customers, classification model is used to predict the behavior of the customers.

Singh et al. (2015) discussed Data mining technique which helps in finding hidden patterns and extracting knowledge from the data. They referred various sources including Journals, online data, books, white papers, conference proceedings and abstracts. They have reviewed a total of 861 research papers and listed 83 of them. They have focussed on the developments in the area of data mining from the year 2007 to 2012, targeting it in association with customer relationship management, association rule mining, data mining algorithms and application areas relating to data mining. The listings mentioned in this paper aims at providing a base framework for customer-centric corporate entities, researchers, academicians who uses data mining techniques and their tools. Data mining offers a wide range of tools and techniques which are used across all sectors of business and industry.

Brito et al. (2014) examined two different approaches i.e. clustering and Sub-group discovery as data mining techniques for customer segmentation. They deployed two algorithms namely: K-Mediods and CN-2 SD to better understand customer's taste and preferences. This led the companies to be more efficient and responsive towards the customer requests and to gain the competitive advantage. This model presented six market segments and 49 rules that helped gain better understanding of customer preferences in a highly customised Fashion manufacturer. They also stated that the approach so developed can be utilised in other market areas as well.

Gordini and Veglio (2014) focussed their research in suggesting the main computational data mining model such as classification decision tree to forecast the precise and exact marketing performance in global organizations in today's competitive world. This paper laid emphasis on the efficiency of computational data mining predictive models in reckoning the probability of customer conversion. The main focus on which firms should concentrate was on the identification of the best marketing activities for their future marketing investments. The emphasized that "Affiliate We Site" was best considered for customer conversion.

Aslam and Ashraf (2014) laid emphasis on need of using data mining algorithms in education mining and discussing the applications for the same in their review paper. They laid stress on various algorithms such as Naive Bayes, C4.5, EM, CART, Apriori, SVM and Page Ranker. Deploying these algorithms, have shown remarkable improvement in strategies like course outline formation, teacher student understanding and high output and turn out ratio.

Haen et al.(2013) investigated the best data mining techniques for predicting the customer profitability in combination to data source. The investigation is based on two types of data: data purchased form a specialised vendor i.e. commercially available data and web data. They concentrated on finding which of these provides the highest accuracy as a profitability input indicator. The results of this paper show bagged decision tree gives consistently higher accuracy and web data give a higher predictive performance in terms of profitability than commercial data, but if both data types are combined together, they rendered the best results. Logistic regression, decision tree and bagged decision tree were the techniques applied in this paper. They stated that bagged decision tree should be given preference over the other two techniques to build a model.

Tudor et al. (2011) highlighted the relevance of the optimization techniques used in the process of data mining along with the predictive models and their relevant field work. It also developed CRM system, which offered new opportunities for a strong and profitable relation between clients and the business. This paper focussed on the implications of using data mining techniques to improve customer retention, response rates, attraction, and cross selling. Also it's helping the companies increase the value of their customers, keeping and attracting the right ones.

Khajvand et al. (2011) focussed on the customer lifetime value (CLV) applications for customer segmentation. They considered Beauty and health Customer data. They clustered the customers into segments using two approaches RFM (Recency, Frequency and Monetary) and Extended RFM parameter using K-means algorithm. For identification of market segments, they clustered the customers into several groups and helped developed marketing strategies for customer retention. They stated that RFM weights vary with the characteristics of industry, so they applied AHP method to find the relative importance of RFM variables based on expert point of view in sale department. On the basis of weighted RFM parameters, they calculated CLV value for each customer segment. On the basis of CLV value, CLV rank was assigned to each segment. The values so generated provided the cross selling opportunities based on financial viewpoint and potential value. By analyzing the CLV rank of segmented customer groups, refined marketing strategies for each segment were developed.

Ngai et al. (2009) analysed the academic literature of the applications of data mining to CRM. Between 2002-2006, they covered 24 journals which provided an academic database of literature and further proposed a classification scheme for the classification of articles. A total of 900 papers were found and reviewed, of which 87 selected papers were classified into four different dimensions of CRM and seven functions of data mining (Clustering, forecasting, association, Regression, Sequence discovery and Visualisation). They aim to provide a research summary on the applications of data mining techniques in CRM domains which are most often used. Their results stated that majority of the reviewed articles were related to customer retention and the research in this area is likely to increase in further coming years.

2.4 RECOMMENDER SYSTEMS(RS)

RS helps in identifying useful items from large search areas to form community opinions. RS have attracted much attention in a past decade and have paved a way for various industries in identifying interesting terms. RS came into existence with the development of web 2.0. There are many recommender systems available today, both in industry and academia. Today RS like diversity focused recommenders and novelty focused recommenders etc are prevalent in the market. Diversity focused systems lays stress on increasing the diversity of the recommendations by utilizing methods like network based collaborative filtering, selective predictability etc. Collaborative RS are more prone to profile injection attacks. To get the desired output, fake profiles are inserted into the database by the malicious users.

Zhang (2014) proposed an online method by combining Hilbert Huang transform (HHT) and Support vector machine (SVM) methods to identify these online profile injection attacks. While novelty based recommender presented a content based recommender, which makes use of text documents containing description of the items and helps in measuring the similarity between them. Recently, implementation of RS has increased, which has facilitated its use in the diverse areas. The huge amount of literature is focused on different topics like movies, music, e-learning, e-commerce, web search among others. More studies of RS are focused on movie recommendations, consisting of large volume of research papers. Recently, RS was designed and implemented to run in Android based multimedia device. It recommended movies to the users according to their profile and previous ratings by Martinez et al in 2015. It also recommended content to the user available either online or locally.

Gavials et al (2013) utilized RS to offer travelling recommendations to the tourists and classifying mobile tourism RS. In March 2014, personal HRS was proposed and used to centralize an individual's health data and provided access to individuals and personalized health officials. In this paper Hybrid recommender system is presented; a combination of both Collaborative filtering, artificial intelligence and data analytics. Despite of the rising attention for various RS, there are still few areas like E-commerce, sciences etc where these recommender systems need to be addressed properly.

2.5 SIMILARITY FINDING

In Earlier days, collaborative filtering method has been implemented in diverse fields like Medical, Online Social platforms, Travel Industry, Hotel reservation, analyzing financial data, Identifying Global trends and many more.

Nguyen et al. (2019) used advanced cosine similarity method for different variants in Collaborative filtering and proposed a triangle measure area as an improved version for cosine measure.

Sandhu et al (2016) proposed a framework to find similarity for dengue disease using CBR and domain thesaurus.

Lahitani et al. (2016) proposed a framework for measuring similarity in a document by using cosine similarity a TF_IDF method. They conducted test on different Indonesian text-based documents that underwent the pre-processing step for extracting the data.

Chen et al. (2014) implemented collaborative filtering method to generate recommendations for reservations in Hotel with the help of keywords and those keywords indicated various user preferences or choices.

Rao et al. (2012) predicted a diagnosis of a disease in real time based on intelligence and thus reducing the false positives and false negatives of a disease. Similarly various methods have been proposed to measure similarity between various objects in different domains like Health care, Image retrieval etc.

CHAPTER 3: PRESENT WORK

3.1 GAP ANALYSIS

We humans have been referring to the term artificial intelligence in today's world and not all people actually know what Artificial Intelligence is? And why it is needed in the modern era. At the same time people are not aware that in the current scenario, this Artificial Intelligence is everywhere in the modern world. For every decade, there is an unforeseen rise in the population. And the secret truth we need to realize is that we are already using Artificial Intelligence. But people still assume that the concept is new, and we now have to apply it. And the prime reason we need artificial intelligence inculcated in our daily lives is because of the population.

As day by day, the population is growing and the client's needs are often increasing from day-to-day. So in a given period of time, the organisation can't afford to fulfil the on-demand customer requirement today. So, they need an alternative in this case. This alternative is the use of Artificial Intelligence that we have today. AI can help automate the task. This saves the organisation's manpower and improves productivity as well. In addition, with the help of Artificial Intelligence, the organisation can also hunt for the people eligible for the company's growth. Furthermore, today's businesses claim that they want to mechanise all the daily and repetitive jobs.

With the passing time and evolving techniques for Artificial intelligence, there are significant changes associated with research methods and methods of application. For example, the system in CRM consists of automating tasks, increasing sales, customer satisfaction, delivering products, understanding user behaviour and making predictions. More data collection costs were involved in the previous approaches conducted in the E-commerce sector, and the productivity needed to build research designs was difficult to implement. In earlier times, Recommendation process only helped to recommend various products or services in their respective domains. It was a hard process to find similar products with the same problem. Many research papers on e-commerce products have been written stating their services, their pricing-related recommendations, but hardly any research work has been done to suggest similar products to consumers based on the purchase count and make predictions for the same. It is important to understand the consumer behaviour and then find the best suited product as per their need. Appropriate use of user data helps to reveal recent information about the customers ' needs and makes it easier for companies and marketing teams to respond at the right time to upcoming issues and requirements. However, the growth in the volume of data in the field of e-commerce has accelerated the data processing framework's storage capacity. So an AI helps to identify and suggest similar products and make predictions for the same behaviour while at the same time understand the user behaviour.

3.2 PROBLEM FORMULATION

In the post digitalisation era, CRM could complete its tasks in a simpler way, just with the help of a database. However, till today, information management has been a tedious activity and has focused primarily on gathering, preserving and supplying customers with data as per their request. Although the essential tasks such as the knowledge extraction, review and interpretation process that makes knowledge a valuable commodity, have not been considered.

In the past 2-3 decades, competition has increased enormously and swiftly, which in turn has increased pressure on companies to be nimble-footed and receptive. CRM helps serve their customers better by studying their buying behaviour, usage patterns etc. With more awareness and knowledge, customers look for personalised experienced at affordable prices and with high-quality service. CRM's primary objective is to understand clients, their expectations and to provide them with personalised and useful items. Earlier CRM was observed as a mere repository only for data from a consumer. In conjunction with ever-increasing data volumes, an enterprise requires AI with CRM to adapt and execute digital transformation. To stay ahead of the competition in businesses, they need to prioritize customer care, customer satisfaction and loyalty and for this, CRM software has to provide with faster and better solutions complementing the human efforts.

A CRM is like a needle in a haystack without AI, machine learning and predictive analysis. CRM software with infused-AI will help organizations to prioritize audiences, alerting them to make a purchase of the products that have the highest proclivity (Rao et al. 2012). With AI, customer's need can be better anticipated even without having to pick up their phone. AI driven CRM can help organizations constantly monitor their customer's status, their needs and can automatically notify the correct person based on their statuses, thereby eliminating the chances of customer slipping through the cracks (Matty 2017).

Earlier days witnessed, whenever a customer calls a customer care agent regarding queries, the entire customer profile was analyzed by the agent before answering them. This is time-consuming process and diminishes the interaction rate between the customer and the customer care agent. Even there are many cases where customers disconnect the call weary of waiting for a long time. By integrating AI into this system, a major transformation is taking place in the era of CRM. With AI's astute data analysis ability, it takes a fraction of second to analyze the individual customer profiles with greater precision and perfection thereby reducing time and enabling better interaction. Moreover, it will help agent by providing them the righteous Input at the right time so that they can respond to customer queries in a more informed fashion. Additionally AI can help enable automated services to customers, to predict their interests based on their online history and to enable productive experience by sending timely notifications.

The growth of AI presents businesses platforms with variety of unique benefits and opportunities. It can empower organizations to provide more relevant and better experiences to their customers and build long-term relations with them that were simply not possible before. With the creation of new relationship between man and machine, A.I. could boost labor productivity to much greater extent and doubling the annual economic growth rates by 2035.

3.2.1 Objectives

1) To generate a repository of Customer data through data analytics.
2) To develop an algorithm to generate purchase recommendations and purchase predictions.
3) To predict Online behaviour and targeting customer base by publicising using predictive analysis/data analytics.
4) To compare the developed virtual assistant in respond to business services.

CHAPTER 4

PROPOSED WORK FOR RECOMMENDING PRODUCTS

Figure 4.1 below demonstrates the proposed system for recommending products and predicting their purchase behavior.

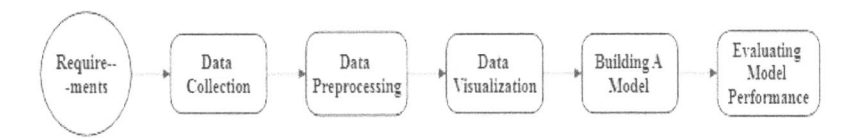

Figure 4.1: Proposed Model for Product recommendation

This model will generate recommendation list based on a specified user, such as:

- INPUT: Visitor 0ID(Customer ID)
- OUTPUT: Product Ids, (Items or Products that the customer is most likely to buy and put in his/her empty basket.)

4.1 DATA COLLECTION

This is the first step in the process of framework. Data has been collected from real-world e-commerce website under an integrated Database. It is a raw data. The dataset consists of four different files: events.csv depicting the behavioural data of the customers, itemproperties1.csv and itemproperties2.csv depicting the item properties of the customers and a file describing category tree named categorytree.csv. The behavioral data comprises of events like no of clicks, add to cart items, transactions carried out and represents interactions which were accumulated over a period of 4.5

months. There are three types of events a visitor may perform, i.e. "view", "addtocart" or "transaction".

4.2 PURCHASE RECOMMENDATION

Algorithm 1 states the steps for recommending products to the user for purchasing.

Algorithm 1: Algorithm for Purchase Recommendation
Step I: Preprocess the data. *Step II*: Prepare a data as per the count of products purchased by each user. *Step III*: User-item matrix is created to calculate the purchase count of each item. *Step IV*: Training model is prepared and data is split into train and test data *Step V*.1: Then cosine similarity model is applied to compare its performance with already defined baseline model *Step VI*: The developed model is evaluated using RMSE, precision and recall methods. *Step VII*: Exit

This component helps generate recommendations to different user based on their similarity interest. After the data is collected, then the proposed system prepares the data on the basis of number of products purchased by each user and forms a user-item matrix. It then applies similarity finding method to extract the similarity between different users and their interests.

4.3 SIMILARITY FINDING (COSINE SIMILARITY)

Cosine similarity is defined as a way to measure the degree of similarity between two n-dimensional vectors in n-dimensional space. It is calculated by the cosine of the angle between two vectors and helps find whether those two vectors are in same direction or not. It has been mostly used to measure similarity within documents in text analysis. This is a conventional approach that is coupled with the TF-IDF. It is represented as a dot product of two vectors divided by magnitude of the product of two vectors as stated by Nguyen and Amer (2019).

Figure 2 demonstrates the measuring similarity level of customer's choice using principle of cosine degree; in which vector represents as a customer and a cosine degree between vectors is a degree of similarity. Based on cosine principal, cosine Θ can be either 1 or less than 1 to the value of another angle, then the value of the similarity of the two vectors are said to be similar, when the value of the cosine similarity is 1.

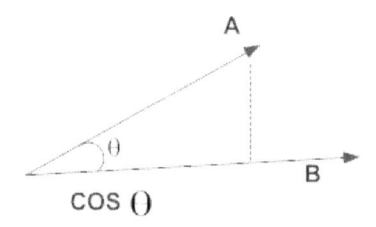

.

$$A$$

$$\theta$$

$$B$$

COS ()

Figure 4.2: Similarity concept by cosine degree

The Results of Weighting term are used for calculating similarity among different customers depending on the products purchased by them. The similarity is used for data classification process having similar characteristics or traits. Similarity concept is used to measure the depth of the similarity among two things considered for comparison and can help enhance the accuracy of information retrieval as discussed by Nguyen and Amer (2019). The technique used to measure the depth of similarity is defined as cosine similarity. This approach is used to identify data with a certain similarity measure based on the number of items (Bobadilla et al. 2009). In other words, Cosine similarity is used for calculating the cosine angle between the numbers of vector of the documents. Using cosine as a similarity function, it is defined as:

$$similarity\,(P,Q) = \frac{P.Q}{\|P\| \times \|Q\|} = \frac{\sum_{i=1}^{n} P_i \times Q_i}{\sqrt{\sum_{i=1}^{n} P_i^2} \times \sqrt{\sum_{i=1}^{n} Q_i^2}}$$

The cosine similarity mainly focuses on the similarity angles between two different things. The users are said to be similar if their preference vectors lies close to a distance measure. Closer the vectors are, smaller will be the angle between them, thus larger the cosine value. In this, we'll calculate the similarity between each pair of different products or items. It helps to find the similarity score between the users. On the basis of this similarity score, algorithm 2 will pick the most similar items and recommends products to the similar users which they have recently bought or liked.

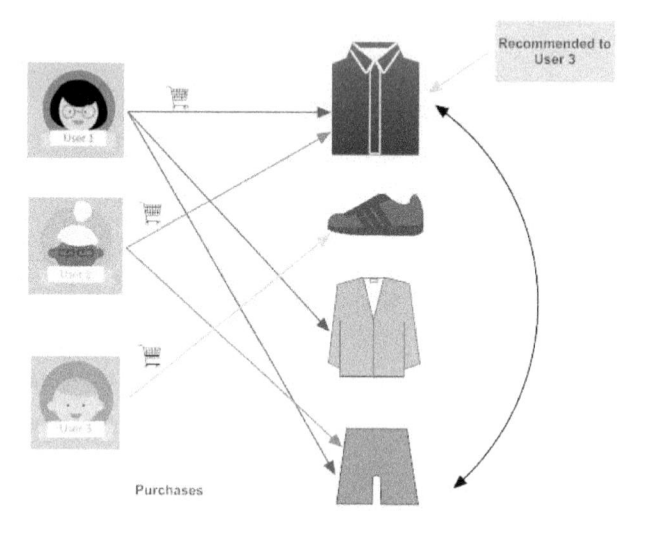

Figure 4.3: Collaborative Filtering Technique

Collaborative filtering technique is the main technique under which cosine similarity is implemented. This technique helps to render the recommendation to the user in an effective way. Figure 4.3 depicts the working of collaborative filtering technique.

Algorithm 2: Algorithm for Similarity Finder across users (Cosine similarity)
Step I:. Create user-item similarity matrix. *Step II:* Find the products purchased by both the users and based on their purchased history, correlation between the users is calculated. *Step III:* To Calculate the similarity between products P and Q: *Step III i:* Look for all users 1 and 2 who have rated both these items P and Q. *Step IV:* Two item-vectors are created, v1 for P and v2 for Q in the user space of 1and 2. *Step V:* The Distance/cosine angle is calculated between these vectors. *Step V i:* An overlapping vectors or zero angle with cosine value 1 results in total Similarity (or there is same rating per user across all items) *Step Vii:* If vectors have 90 degree angle between them with cosine value 0, it results in no similarity. *Step VI:* For each user, predict the purchase count of the products that he had bought earlier or the probability to buy a product. *Step VI i:* Calculate the rating for a user 2 of the target item, say X using above calculated similarity measure among the target item and already bought other items. It is calculated on the basis of purchase counts. *StepVI ii:* Thus predicted rating for item 'P' for user 2 is calculated using similarity measures. *Step V*IIs: Exit

4.4 EXPERIMENTAL SETUP AND PERFORMANCE ANALYSIS FOR RECOMMENDING PRODUCTS

After a comprehensive internet search, we found a dataset on Kaggle for e-commerce websites. We will be using these datasets to perform our proposed architecture. Experimental setup and performance analysis for is divided into three main components which are:

4.4.1 Data Pre-processing

4.4.2 Train and testing data

4.4.3 Recommending Products

4.4.1 Data Pre-processing

This step processes the whole data as per the relevancy required to make product recommendations. Preprocessing is required to form datasets for analysis purpose. Total 27, 56,101 events are there in the dataset of which 26, 64,312 are views by the customers, 69,332 are add to carts events and 22,457 are transactions conducted by 14,07,580 unique visitors. Around 90% of events corresponding properties are available in the "item_properties.csv" files.

For example:

- "1549694000000,1,view,100," means visitorId = 1, clicked the item with id = 100 at 1549694000000 (Unix timestamp)
- "1549694000000,2,transaction,1000,234" means visitorId = 2 purchased the item with id = 1000 in transaction with id = 234 at 1549694000000 (Unix timestamp)

The item_properties.csv file consists of item properties having 20,275,902 rows out of which 4, 17,053 are unique items. File has been divided into 2 parts because of its file size limitations. Every row has a different timestamp because the property of an item can vary with time, for example price changes over time. In other words, different snapshots of every week are attached in the file along with the behaviour data. However, if a property of an item is constant over the observed period, only a single snapshot value is present in the file.

For example, below Figure 4.4 and Figure 4.5 are the descriptions of three properties for single item and four weekly merged snapshots respectively:

```
timestamp,itemid,property,value
1439694000000,1,100,1000
1439695000000,1,100,1000
1439696000000,1,100,1000
1439697000000,1,100,1000
1439694000000,1,200,1000
1439695000000,1,200,1100
1439696000000,1,200,1200
1439697000000,1,200,1300
1439694000000,1,300,1000
1439695000000,1,300,1000
1439696000000,1,300,1100
1439697000000,1,300,1100
```

Figure 4.4: Snapshot for Single Item

```
1439694000000,1,100,1000
1439694000000,1,200,1000
1439695000000,1,200,1100
1439696000000,1,200,1200
1439697000000,1,200,1300
1439694000000,1,300,1000
1439696000000,1,300,1100
```

Figure 4.5: Snapshot for merged four weekly items

Item properties file consists of timestamp column as properties such as price; category, etc. are time dependent and can vary with time. Initially, every week's snapshots were included in the events file and made up of about 200 million rows. Subsequently, consecutive constant property values were combined and transformed from snapshot form to log form to allow constant values appear in the file only once. This conversion has enormously minimized the row count by 10 times.

Hashing was applied on all the attributes in the "item_properties.csv" file except for "categoryid" and "available" properties to normalise the text values. "categoryid" property contains the value as item category identifier. "available" property value implies that the item is available, i.e. 0 instructs the item is not available and vice versa as1. At the beginning, the numerical values were started with "n" char and have precision of 3 digits after decimal point, e.g., "7" is "n7.000", "-2.76584" will be "n-2.7658". Using stemming and hashing, all text values are normalised. All numbers have been processed as above. Example: text "The world 2020!" will result to "214 44214 n2020.000". The schema of four different csv files i.e. category id, Event, item_properties_part1 and item_properties_part2 are respectively represented below in Table 4.1:

Table 4.1: The first schema refers to Category database containing only two attributes, whereas second schema corresponds to events database which consist of three different types of events namely; add to cart, view and bought while third and fourth schema corresponds to item properties

Categoryid			Parentid		
Timestamp	Visitorid	Itemid		Transaction_id	Event
Timestamp		Itemid		Property	Value
Timestamp		Itemid		Property	Value

Clustering was performed on the data to extract the buying visitors and viewing visitors. Then an array was created for both buyers and visitor's list. The buying list and viewer's list of customers along with the products viewed is displayed below in Figure 4.6 and Figure 4.7 respectively.

	visitorid	items_viewed	items_bought	count	purchased
0	172	[465522, 10034, 107943, 79918, 62300, 202268, ...	[465522, 10034]	2	1
1	186	[49029]	[49029]	1	1
2	264	[459835, 161949]	[459835, 161949]	2	1
3	419	[19278, 426926, 46391]	[19278]	1	1
4	539	[94371]	[94371]	1	1

Figure 4.6: Customer who purchased the products

	visitorid	items_viewed	items_bought	count	purchased
0	523483	[56441, 339703, 42457, 380165, 342443]	[]	0	0
1	1242849	[115693, 127608]	[]	0	0
2	488234	[336543]	[]	0	0
3	555254	[305646]	[]	0	0
4	433661	[413166]	[]	0	0

Figure 4.7: Customers who viewed the products

A table is prepared as input for modeling purpose which consists of visitor id, product id and purchase_count for each product purchased as shown in figure 4.8.

	visitorid	productId	purchase_count
0	172	10034	1
1	172	465522	1
2	186	49029	1
3	264	161949	1
4	264	459835	1

Figure 4.8: Input table prepared for modelling

Then user-item matrix is prepared to normalize purchase count of each product across users as given in the figure 4.9 below:

productId	15	19	25	42	147	168	199	212	233	304	...	466319	466321	466342	466443	466464	466526	466603	466614	466710	466861
visitorid																					
172	NaN	NaN	NaN	NaN	NaN	NaN	NaN	NaN	NaN	NaN	...	NaN	NaN	NaN	NaN	NaN	NaN	NaN	NaN	NaN	NaN
186	NaN	NaN	NaN	NaN	NaN	NaN	NaN	NaN	NaN	NaN	...	NaN	NaN	NaN	NaN	NaN	NaN	NaN	NaN	NaN	NaN
264	NaN	NaN	NaN	NaN	NaN	NaN	NaN	NaN	NaN	NaN	...	NaN	NaN	NaN	NaN	NaN	NaN	NaN	NaN	NaN	NaN
419	NaN	NaN	NaN	NaN	NaN	NaN	NaN	NaN	NaN	NaN	...	NaN	NaN	NaN	NaN	NaN	NaN	NaN	NaN	NaN	NaN
539	NaN	NaN	NaN	NaN	NaN	NaN	NaN	NaN	NaN	NaN	...	NaN	NaN	NaN	NaN	NaN	NaN	NaN	NaN	NaN	NaN
...	...	...	...	...	...	...	...	...	...	...	...	...	...	...	...	...	...	...	...	...	...
1406787	NaN	NaN	NaN	NaN	NaN	NaN	NaN	NaN	NaN	NaN	...	NaN	NaN	NaN	NaN	NaN	NaN	NaN	NaN	NaN	NaN
1406981	NaN	NaN	NaN	NaN	NaN	NaN	NaN	NaN	NaN	NaN	...	NaN	NaN	NaN	NaN	NaN	NaN	NaN	NaN	NaN	NaN
1407070	NaN	NaN	NaN	NaN	NaN	NaN	NaN	NaN	NaN	NaN	...	NaN	NaN	NaN	NaN	NaN	NaN	NaN	NaN	NaN	NaN
1407110	NaN	NaN	NaN	NaN	NaN	NaN	NaN	NaN	NaN	NaN	...	NaN	NaN	NaN	NaN	NaN	NaN	NaN	NaN	NaN	NaN
1407398	NaN	NaN	NaN	NaN	NaN	NaN	NaN	NaN	NaN	NaN	...	NaN	NaN	NaN	NaN	NaN	NaN	NaN	NaN	NaN	NaN

11719 rows × 12025 columns

Figure 4.9: User-Item matrix

4.4.2 Training and Testing data

The most crucial part of evaluating recommender modelling is to split the data into train and test set. Larger portion of the data is considered for training part and smaller portion for testing. A ratio of 70:30 is used for train-test size in our model. Training part is used to develop a recommender model whereas the testing part is used for evaluation of the model and the dataset is divided as shown in figure 4.10.

visitorid	productId	purchase_count	visitorid	productId	purchase_count
270464	77742	1	76757	412516	1
597416	259227	1	474972	440677	1
239974	72721	1	1323154	29757	1
695025	246555	1	346597	133472	1
198270	207178	1	1165148	179784	1
185564	346283	1	134360	273041	1
894065	396633	1	1375685	85791	1
64931	390824	1	830875	267641	1
1356496	248676	1	63181	379520	1
1096676	126851	1	1341635	238928	1

Figure 4.10: Train & Test Sets

4.4.3 Recommending Products

The proposed algorithms is performed on Turicreate system with minimum 4GB RAM and i9 Intel core processor with 2.8 GHz processing power. Each user having similar preferences is compared based on different products purchased and ten product recommendations are made to each user. Proposed product recommender is compared with the popularity baseline recommender algorithm (Bressan et al. 2016). Train and Test sets created by the pre-processing of the data serve as an input to these two algorithms. All algorithms are run and comparison is done on various parameters such as Root mean Square Error (RMSE), Recall and precision values.

4.5 RESULTS AND DISCUSSION

Proposed Model is simple and still effectual to find similar users and recommending products between different users with the help of collaborative filtering cosine measure. It involves collecting data for e-commerce website and data pre-processing as per the model's requirement. Data was segregated in two forms-one buyers list and second viewer's list. It was then normalized and combined to form user-item matrix. Secondly, it includes creation of train and test sets by splitting the data on 70:30 ratios. Then target variables were defined in turicreate model and similar users were found and were recommended ten products each to all users based on their preferences. Recommended products to the users are shown in the figure 4.11. The Evaluation of proposed architecture is performed on metrics such as RMSE, Recall and precision as shown in the figure 4.12(a) and 4.12(b). The time taken to respond to the system by the servers is referred to as response time. It looks for the first response received from the servers to the proposed system. Trained data is given as input to both our proposed system and popularity based (baseline) algorithm to check for response time. As depicted in the Figure 4.13, the response time of the training set in proposed algorithm is better than the popularity based (baseline) algorithm and proposed algorithm recommends products better than popularity based (baseline) algorithm because baseline algorithm recommends only the same top products to all the users. RMSE help calculate the error of recommended values and thus lower the RMSE value better is the recommendations. Another parameter Recall helps us to know about percentage of products bought by a user that were really recommended to them. For example: if a customer buys 6 products and out of which 3 recommendations were made, then recall is 0.5. Similarly, precision is defined as number of users who actually liked the items from all the recommendations made to them For example: If 6 products were recommended to the user and he buys 4 of them, precision is 0.6.

```
+------------+-----------+------------------------+------+        +------------+-----------+-------+------+
|            |   Cosine Similarity               |      |        |            | Baseline Model        |      |
| visitorid  | productId |         score          | rank |        | visitorid  | productId | score | rank |
+------------+-----------+------------------------+------+        +------------+-----------+-------+------+
|   1164713  |   307306  |  0.1414213538169861    |   1  |        |   1164713  |   52928   |  1.0  |   1  |
|   1164713  |    47352  |  0.1414213538169861    |   2  |        |   1164713  |  301602   |  1.0  |   2  |
|   1164713  |   239974  |  0.1414213538169861    |   3  |        |   1164713  |   80519   |  1.0  |   3  |
|   1164713  |   357529  |  0.1273975372314453    |   4  |        |   1164713  |  208939   |  1.0  |   4  |
|   1164713  |   447067  |  0.11032949686050415   |   5  |        |   1164713  |  443344   |  1.0  |   5  |
|   1164713  |   265082  |  0.08164966106414795   |   6  |        |   1164713  |  127507   |  1.0  |   6  |
|   1164713  |   199279  |  0.08164966106414795   |   7  |        |   1164713  |   96883   |  1.0  |   7  |
|   1164713  |   210993  |  0.08164966106414795   |   8  |        |   1164713  |  207802   |  1.0  |   8  |
|   1164713  |   372523  |  0.08164966106414795   |   9  |        |   1164713  |  396853   |  1.0  |   9  |
|   1164713  |   241876  |  0.08164966106414795   |  10  |        |   1164713  |  315393   |  1.0  |  10  |
|   1182823  |    52928  |          0.0           |   1  |        |   1182823  |   52928   |  1.0  |   1  |
|   1182823  |   301602  |          0.0           |   2  |        |   1182823  |  301602   |  1.0  |   2  |
|   1182823  |    80519  |          0.0           |   3  |        |   1182823  |   80519   |  1.0  |   3  |
|   1182823  |   208939  |          0.0           |   4  |        |   1182823  |  208939   |  1.0  |   4  |
|   1182823  |   443344  |          0.0           |   5  |        |   1182823  |  443344   |  1.0  |   5  |
|   1182823  |   127507  |          0.0           |   6  |        |   1182823  |  127507   |  1.0  |   6  |
|   1182823  |    96883  |          0.0           |   7  |        |   1182823  |   96883   |  1.0  |   7  |
|   1182823  |   207802  |          0.0           |   8  |        |   1182823  |  207802   |  1.0  |   8  |
|   1182823  |   396853  |          0.0           |   9  |        |   1182823  |  396853   |  1.0  |   9  |
|   1182823  |   303229  |          0.0           |  10  |        |   1182823  |  303229   |  1.0  |  10  |
|   152963   |   144211  |  0.011714927296140301  |   1  |        |   152963   |   52928   |  1.0  |   1  |
|   152963   |   329587  |  0.011714927296140301  |   2  |        |   152963   |  301602   |  1.0  |   2  |
|   152963   |   244205  |  0.011714927296140301  |   3  |        |   152963   |   80519   |  1.0  |   3  |
|   152963   |   187405  |  0.011714927296140301  |   4  |        |   152963   |  208939   |  1.0  |   4  |
|   152963   |   380394  |  0.011714927296140301  |   5  |        |   152963   |  443344   |  1.0  |   5  |
|   152963   |   199279  |  0.011714927296140301  |   6  |        |   152963   |  127507   |  1.0  |   6  |
|   152963   |   210993  |  0.011714927296140301  |   7  |        |   152963   |   96883   |  1.0  |   7  |
|   152963   |   372523  |  0.011714927296140301  |   8  |        |   152963   |  207802   |  1.0  |   8  |
|   152963   |   288205  |  0.011714927296140301  |   9  |        |   152963   |  315393   |  1.0  |   9  |
|   152963   |   356696  |  0.011714927296140301  |  10  |        |   152963   |  303229   |  1.0  |  10  |
+------------+-----------+------------------------+------+        +------------+-----------+-------+------+
```

Figure 4.11: Comparison between Proposed Algorithm and Popularity based (baseline) Algorithm

Baseline Model

Overall RMSE: 0.9972301788673194

Per User RMSE (best)

```
+-----------+----------------------+-------+
| visitorid |         rmse         | count |
+-----------+----------------------+-------+
|   390023  |  0.2928932309150696  |   1   |
+-----------+----------------------+-------+
```
[1 rows x 3 columns]

Per User RMSE (worst)

```
+-----------+------+-------+
| visitorid | rmse | count |
+-----------+------+-------+
|   566725  |  1.0 |   1   |
+-----------+------+-------+
```
[1 rows x 3 columns]

Per Item RMSE (best)

```
+-----------+----------------------+-------+
| productId |         rmse         | count |
+-----------+----------------------+-------+
|   361945  |  0.1835033893585205  |   1   |
+-----------+----------------------+-------+
```
[1 rows x 3 columns]

Per Item RMSE (worst)

```
+-----------+------+-------+
| productId | rmse | count |
+-----------+------+-------+
|   247427  |  1.0 |   1   |
+-----------+------+-------+
```
[1 rows x 3 columns]

Cosine Similarity

Overall RMSE: 0.0

Per User RMSE (best)

```
+-----------+------+-------+
| visitorid | rmse | count |
+-----------+------+-------+
|  1044862  |  0.0 |   1   |
+-----------+------+-------+
```
[1 rows x 3 columns]

Per User RMSE (worst)

```
+-----------+------+-------+
| visitorid | rmse | count |
+-----------+------+-------+
|   566725  |  0.0 |   1   |
+-----------+------+-------+
```
[1 rows x 3 columns]

Per Item RMSE (best)

```
+-----------+------+-------+
| productId | rmse | count |
+-----------+------+-------+
|   331910  |  0.0 |   1   |
+-----------+------+-------+
```
[1 rows x 3 columns]

Per Item RMSE (worst)

```
+-----------+------+-------+
| productId | rmse | count |
+-----------+------+-------+
|   247427  |  0.0 |   1   |
+-----------+------+-------+
```
[1 rows x 3 columns]

Figure 4.12(a): RMSE of Proposed algorithm and Popularity based (baseline) algorithm

```
Precision and recall summary statistics of Cosine Similarity
+--------+------------------------+------------------------+
| cutoff |     mean_precision     |      mean_recall       |
+--------+------------------------+------------------------+
|   1    |  0.008801141769743098  |  0.006776709256490413  |
|   2    |  0.004995242626070412  |  0.007643230936523043  |
|   3    |  0.003488740881699697  |  0.007724785918173173  |
|   4    |  0.002794957183634634  |  0.008319457659372030  |
|   5    |  0.002331113225499525  |  0.008458214398985088  |
|   6    |  0.002140818268315894  |  0.009310577228036795  |
|   7    |  0.001902949571836347  |  0.009667380272756102  |
|   8    |  0.001724548049476688  |  0.010024183317475422  |
|   9    |  0.001559361454699227  |  0.010063828100222003  |
|   10   |  0.001427212178877259  |  0.010182762448461778  |
+--------+------------------------+------------------------+

Precision and recall summary statistics of Baseline Model
+--------+------------------------+------------------------+
| cutoff |     mean_precision     |      mean_recall       |
+--------+------------------------+------------------------+
|   1    |         0.0            |         0.0            |
|   2    |         0.0            |         0.0            |
|   3    |         0.0            |         0.0            |
|   4    |         0.0            |         0.0            |
|   5    |         0.0            |         0.0            |
|   6    |  3.964478274659055e-05 |  7.92895654931811e-05  |
|   7    |  6.796248470844094e-05 |  0.00031715826197272444|
|   8    |  5.946717411988584e-05 |  0.00031715826197272241|
|   9    |  5.285971032878735e-05 |  0.00031715826197272444|
|   10   |  4.757373929590866e-05 |  0.00031715826197272444|
+--------+------------------------+------------------------+
```

Figure 4.12(b): Precision- Recall summary of proposed algorithm & Popularity based (baseline) Algorithm

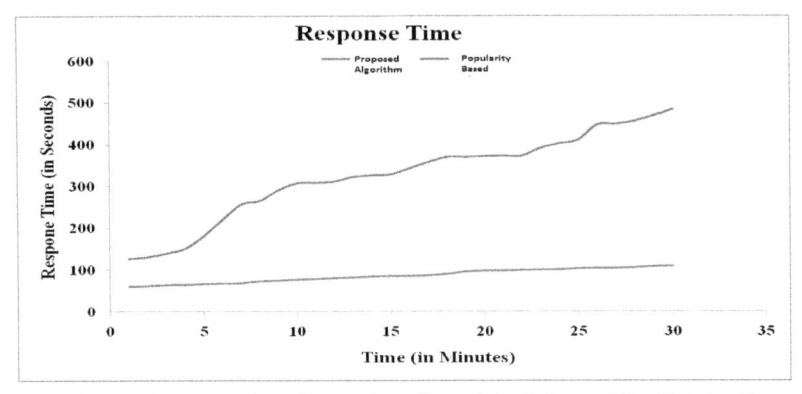

Figure 4.13: Response Time of Proposed algorithm and Popularity based (Baseline) algorithm

CHAPTER 5

PROPOSED WORK FOR PREDICTING PURCHASES

This paper proposes a model for predicting purchases based on a client's purchasing journey from doing window shopping to making a transaction. Figure 5.1 suggests the proposed model for making purchase predictions.

Data visualization component is included after the products are recommended to the users, we need to predict whether or not a users will purchase a product after viewing it.

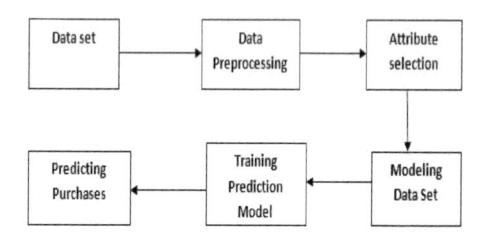

Figure 5.1: Proposed model for Purchase Prediction

5.1 DATA COLLECTION

Dataset was obtained from Kaggle for a period of approximately 4.5 months. In particular we have used four dataset files as illustrated in the Table 3. Since we want to predict the future predictions for the customers whether they will buy a product or not based on their buying journey from viewing to transaction (making purchase). Description of the data is aforementioned in 4.1 and 4.4.1.

Table 5.1: Description of all Dataset files

| Category.csv | Events.csv | Item_Property1.csv | Item_property2.csv |

5.2 A RANDOM FOREST CLASSIFIER

A random forest is defined as an ensemble method (on the basis of divide-and-conquer strategy) in machine learning which includes growing (construction) of multiple Decision trees (DT) via bagging (boot strap aggregation). They are better known as bagged DT's (Shaikhina et al. 2019). In other words, it is a forest comprising of multiple trees and those trees acts as predictors such that each tree acts as a predictor and selects the best possible solution by voting. DT's are created by selecting random data samples, gets prediction from each tree as input and choose the best solution as depicted in the figure 5.2. Random forest has enormous applications such as feature selection, Image classification and recommendation engines. The individual decision trees are created for each attribute using an attribute selection indicator such as data gain, gain ratio and Gini index.

Algorithm 3: Algorithm for Random Forest Classifier

Step I:. Select random features "h" from a given dataset "k" such that h<<k.

Step II: Amongst the h features, node "d" is calculated with the help of best split point.

Step III: Then the daughter node is build from the root node using best split

Step IV: Repeat I-III steps till "m" nodes are reached.

Step V: Forest is built by repeating steps I-IV for "n" times for creating "n" trees.

Step V: Exit

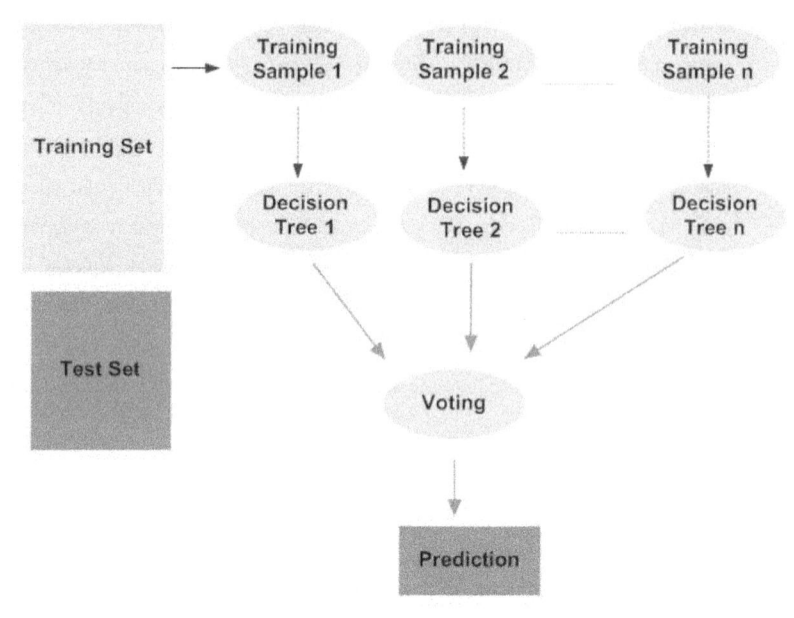

Figure 5.2: Random Forest Prediction Model

After the Random forest classifier is built based on the decision trees using algorithm 3, next step is to generate predictions. Algorithm 4 explains the Random forest prediction in detail.

Algorithm 4: Algorithm for Predicting Purchase by Random Forest Classifier

Step I: Preprocess the data.

Step II: Select the attribute or test features

Step III:. Apply Rules based on randomly created decision trees

*Ste*p III: Look for the view_count of the products.

Step IV: Build a train and test data.

Step V: For each predicted target, votes are calculated.

Step V.1: For Final Prediction, maximum voted predicted target is considered among the Random forest Algorithm

Step VII: Exit

5.3 EXPERIMENTAL SET UP FOR PREDICTING PURCHASE
5.3.1 Data Pre-Processing
This step processes data as per the requirements of predicting future purchases. Aforementioned in section 4.4.1, is the total no of rows, the unique data visitors, viewers list and no of customers who purchased the product. Data was not available in specified order, so new amalgamations were created to obtain meaningful data. Clustering of data was conducted to separate the viewer's data from purchase data as discussed in the above section 4.4.1. Buying journey of a customer is represented from viewing to transaction (making purchase) in Figure 5.3. Depending upon their choice or preferences, ten products were recommended to each user as discussed in section 4.4.3 having similar preferences and were compared based on different products purchased. After recommending products to the users, buyer's list and viewer's list were again merged. As we have categorical features in this dataset. So we applied general encoding of all categorical features, thus used the one-hot encoding method for this.

5.3.2 Attribute Selection
This phase includes the selection of attributes, with the aid of which the training and test data will be framed. Visitor ID, items viewed, view count, bought count for a consumer, and whether or not a product is purchased will be used from the selected data as different attributes.

	visitorid	num_items_viewed	view_count	bought_count	purchased
25283	414494	1	1	0	0
31516	211489	1	1	0	0
15170	857478	1	1	0	0
10500	1261557	12	15	5	1
35120	1004036	2	2	0	0

Figure 5.3: Attribute selection

5.3.3 Predictive Modelling
At this stage, Decision tree is divided into 3 parts for better understanding and is framed as depicted in the figure 5.4 and the values for the same are evaluated. Random Forest

model is applied on the selected attributes of the customers, with the help of train-test models to predict the future purchase predictions on the list of all the viewers who have visited the website even once for any kind of products. Attributes like visitor id, purchased and bought count having categorical values, were dropped to form train and test data. The complete data was split into train and test set divided in the ratio 70:30. The random forest model was then applied to predict the test characteristics. A binary classification is the effective choice provided in the above context and helps to classify future predictions of purchases. Random forest makes use of Gini index or Mean decrease in impurity (MDI) to compute the significance of each feature. The overall decrease in node impurity can also be described as Gini significance. This can be elaborated as how much the accuracy of a model decreases whenever a variable is dropped. The greater the decline, the more important the variable is. The Receiver operating characteristic (ROC) analysis was performed to test the model.

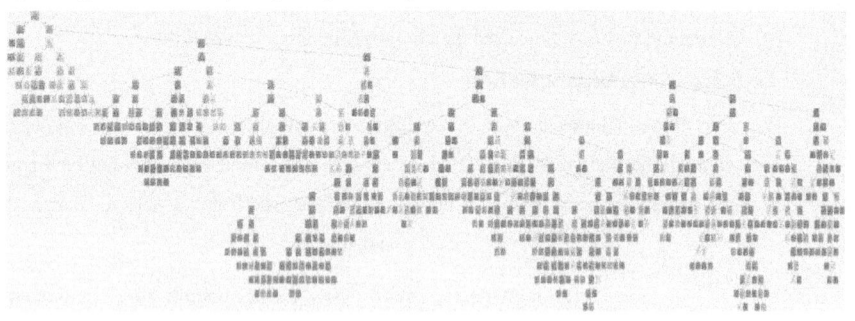

Figure 5.4: Decision Tree formed from random data Samples

5.4 RESULTS

The framework is developed to predict purchase predictions for customers buying any product. The clustered data was again combined to fetch the total of visitors on a website and data was visualised as in figure 5.5. Random forest model was applied on the above framework discussed above. The Accuracy evaluated is against the Logistic regression which is shown in figure 5.6 and 5.7. The model developed is tested with ROC curve.

Our model is more predictive if the ROC line is closer to the top-left side and is graphically shown in figure 5.8 and 5.9. The Results evaluated shows that are proposed system has better accuracy in comparison to Logistic regression

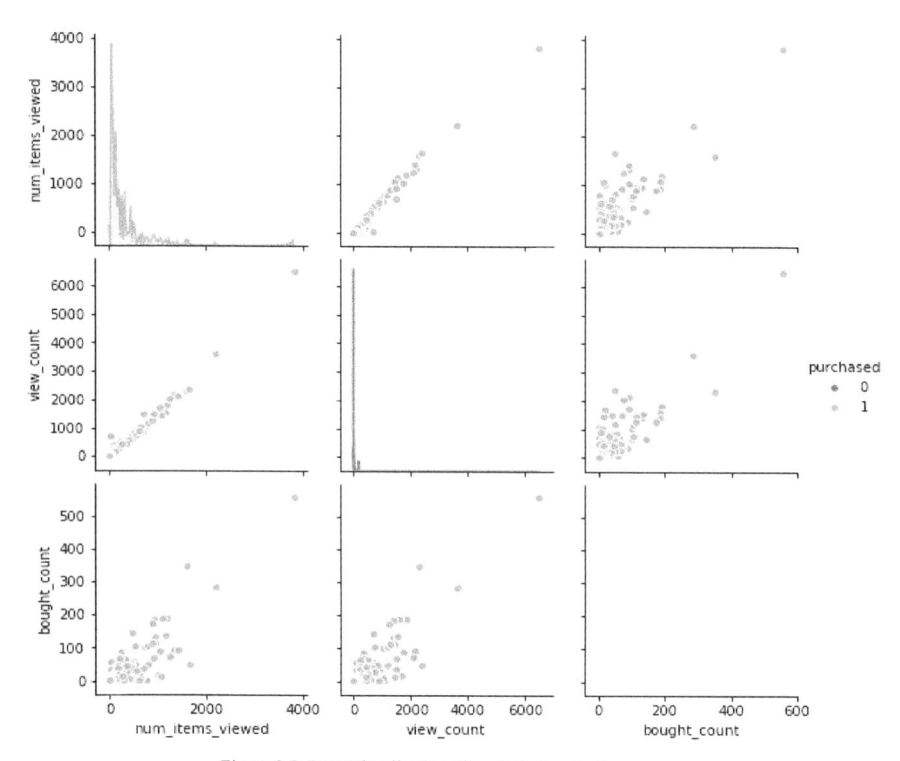

Figure 5.5: Data Visualisation after attribute selection

```
from sklearn.ensemble import RandomForestClassifier
#Running new regression on training data
treeclass = RandomForestClassifier(n_estimators=100)
treeclass.fit(X_train, y_train)
#Calculating the accuracy of the training model on the testing data
y_pred = treeclass.predict(X_test)
y_pred_prob = treeclass.predict_proba(X_test)[:,1]
accuracy = treeclass.score(X_test, y_test)
print('The accuracy is: ' + str(accuracy *100) + '%')

The accuracy is: 81.74001011633788%
```

Figure 5.6: Random Forest Model results

```
LogisticRegression(C=1.0, class_weight=None, dual=False, fit_intercept=True,
                   intercept_scaling=1, l1_ratio=None, max_iter=100,
                   multi_class='auto', n_jobs=None, penalty='l2',
                   random_state=None, solver='lbfgs', tol=0.0001, verbose=0,
                   warm_start=False)
```

```
y_pred_class = logreg.predict(X_test)
```

```
print('accuracy = {:7.4f}'.format(metrics.accuracy_score(y_test, y_pred_class)))

accuracy =  0.7978
```

Figure 5.7: Logistic Regression Results

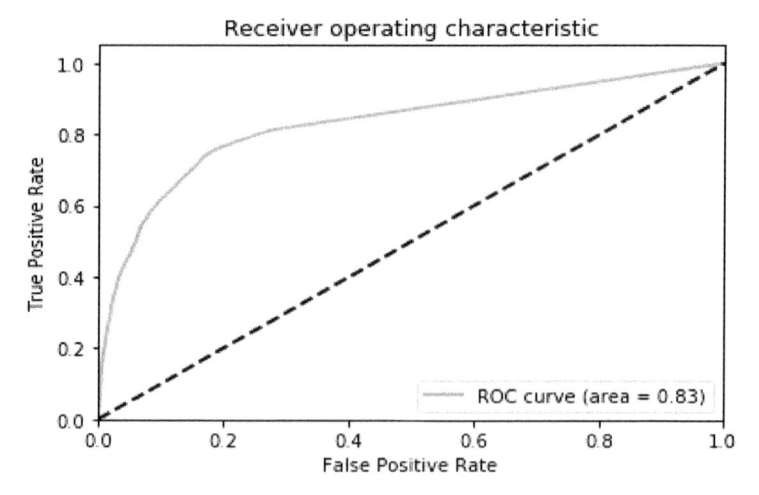

Figure 5.8: Random forest ROC Curve

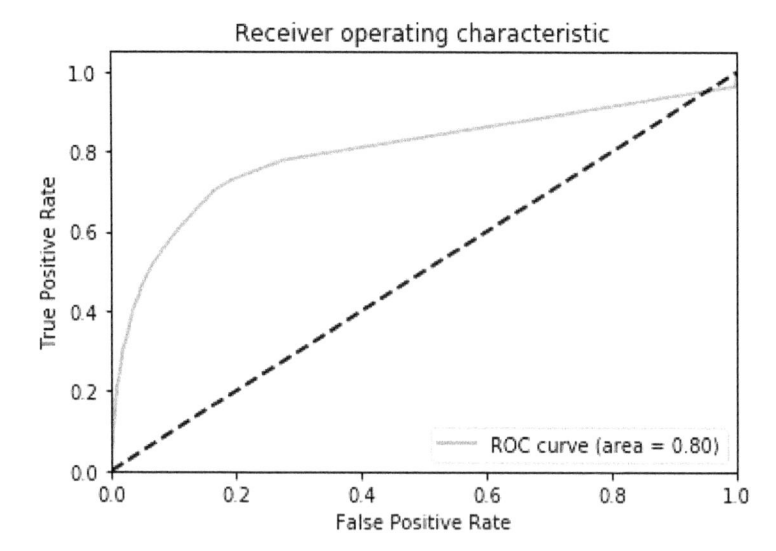

Figure 5.9: Logistic Regression ROC curve

CHAPTER 6

PROPOSED WORK FOR PREDICTING ONLINE BEHAVIOUR OF USERS

The ability to predict the user behavior or intentions for certain product, service offerings or categories on the basis of interactions conducted on a website plays an essential role for e-commerce sites and displaying the relative ads for retargeting. To have a better understanding of the user behavior, it is necessary for online merchants to keep a track of the search patterns of the customers (Sharma & Kumar 2016). Every interaction with any website leaves the digital impression that furnishes the information about the customer's intentions like preferences, interests and the context of visiting the website. Rich amount of data is available in e-commerce websites. The customers does a handful of search regarding the products before making any purchase decision. Various behavior patterns such as search frequency, time spent per product and returning visits, if any, are portrayed by different users (Curme et al. 2014).

By examining the related data, online merchants can actively participate in managing the visitor interactions. A Clickstream in machine learning can be utilized to represent a search behavior, product views, time spent on each product describing the navigational history of any user specially the purchase records (He et al. 2018). Purchasing and search are considered as two essential components which reflect consumers' preferences in some specific category.

Machine learning techniques are used in modern search engines for predicting user's pursuit. The most popular models include Decision trees and Logistic regression. Using a neural network at the top of a logistic regression offers the benefit of capturing a non-linear relationship between input attributes, and its deeper architectures have an inherently enormous modeling power. The Probabilistic generative model articulated with deep neural networks gives an advantage of imitating the customer's purchase behavior and in capturing the latent variables.

This describes the behavior patterns of certain users who are going to make any purchase sessions and generalize the patterns to predict the anticipation of purchase in related websites. The data set includes approximately 1.5 lakh sessions consisting of the data related to clicks done by the user. However, around 2% of the training data consists of information related to buy sessions.

6.1 DATA DESCRIPTION

Data consists of four-five months of user activity logs on the e-commerce website. Attributes include a Visitorid, timestamp and eventtype. The Data consists of mainly 4 types of events: page view of a product, addtocart, transaction and view. There are about 20 000 different categories of products. In either the case of a transaction or an addtocart, the financial information and other details are included. The data is a high dimensional and sparse data. In order to minimize the dimensionality of the data, one of the two ways can be opted: reduction, i.e. average page views per individual over time or average items viewed over a certain period of time. As most shopping (approx 85%) of any product occurs within 6 days of user's first visit, so we opted for first approach.

The training data comprises of a set of sessions $n \in N$ and every session includes a set of products $p \in P$ which as user can see. The products bought by the user in session n are denoted by T_n. There are two types of session belonging to N_t (the session in which transaction was made) and N_{nt} (session in which no transaction was done). Given the set of sessions Ni, main emphasis lies in finding all N_t sessions that have minimum one purchase event. If any session N consists of a purchase event, we would like to predict the products N_t bought in that session. The data includes only 1% of the products (200) for which full category identification is available. However, this chunk of data corresponds to 90% of transactions and 80% of page views which therefore leads to unbalanced distribution. As we have a huge data around 8GB, so it is difficult to load into memory. Therefore considering a sample of around 100 000 events. Snapshot of which is described below:

- 26, 64,312 are pageview events (78% of overall events) from 14,07,580 unique Visitors.
- 69332 addtocart (10%) from 11091 unique users.
- 22457 sales events (2.5 percent) from 2016 distinct users (about 1.1 sales per individual).

Restricting the product label categories to 250, there exists around 139451 pageviews, from 7, 741, 69 unique users, constituting about half of the population. As data is sparse, time was inconsiderable and has been aggregated on various temporal bases as depicted in table below.

Table 6.1: Parameters for Clickstream

Symbol	Description
D_n	Duration of the session prior to any purchase
CL/b	Click to buy ratio
N_B	no of session before any transaction
Ds	Description
Cost	Cost of a product
Time	Amount of time spent on a product
Hr	Hour of the day when session took place
Nc_l	no of clicks in a session
V_{24hr}	page views in past 24hours
V_{week}	Page views in past week

6.2 CLASSIFIERS

The main task in this section is to predict the set of products that will be purchased during that session. Two different sets of classifiers i.e. Binary and ranking prediction were used. The reason for selecting two set of classifiers is due to high dimensionality of the data. The classifiers used for testing the performance are: logistic Regression, Random Forest and Ensemble Method. Standard Area under ROC curve (AUC) is used as a KPI to measure the performance. AUC with the value of 1 is considered as the perfect classifier and 10 cross fold validation is used for conducting execution.

6.2.1 Ensemble Method

Decision trees have some advantageous characteristics over the other classification techniques like linear regression, Support vector machines, Logistic Regression and neural networks. It helps to visualize the structure of the classifier in a better way by representing it graphically. It helps to understand the steps involved in classification process such as the order followed for different variables, which variables are used, etc. Decision trees are considered brisk in classifying data and are trained in relatively short time (Sharma and Kumar 2016). Ensemble Method is a framework for machine learning, where several weak learner models are trained to perform the same task and combined to produce better results. It consists of three meta algorithms, namely: Bagging, Boosting and Stacking.

6.2.1a Bagging with Random Forest Method

The Random Forest (RF) created an ensemble of decision trees with the aid of randomization. The random forest approach is one of the methods of bagging where deep trees are combined to generate an output with reduced variance, equipped on bootstrap samples. It uses sampling over the selected features and uses only a random subset to build a tree (He et al. 2018). The input classification of the trees is done individually whenever any input is classified. The majority votes considered from all the trees helps in deciding the final classification. The average likelihood on the leaves of each tree defines the probability of a certain input per class.

Each tree is cultivated randomly and independently. The subset of the original training data is used to train a tree; therefore, random selections of each training example are made from the original group. At each tree node, instead of checking the best split among all the attributes values, a subset of the attributes is randomly chosen and is considered for deciding the best split. Each tree grows to its maximum extent, which ensures that no pruning occurs. The classifier so obtained is adequate to deal with large data sets which consist of missing data, more number of variables and outliers (Christy et al. 2018). Random forest helps reducing the variance of "complex" models with low bias. The composition elements in this model are not "weak" rather are too complex. The trees underlying it are planted "slightly" as big as "possible." The associated trees are parallel independent models. In addition to it, a random variable is added to trees to make them even more independent, that improves their performance even better than ordinary bagging and thus it is entitled as "random."

6.2.1b Boosting

In the same spirit as bagging methods, boosting methods work: we create a class of models which are aggregated to get a strong learner which performs better. However, unlike bagging that mostly seeks to minimize variance, boosting technique laid emphasis on fitting multiple weak learners sequentially in a very adaptive way. Boosting can be implemented to both Classification and Regression problems. We have two most important boosting algorithms: Adaboost and Gradient boosting. Base model consisting of trees is considered for boosting as it has low variance but high biasing.

6.3 DEEP NEURAL NETWORK

Deep learning describes a wide range of machine learning methods and frameworks with the characteristic of utilizing several non-linear layers of hierarchical computation (Kiarashinejad et al. 2020). The idea of deep learning emerged from research on the MLPs with several hidden layers related to as deep neural networks (DNNs) or artificial neural network-feed-forward neural networks. Such networks are usually equipped by a Back-propagation (BP) known as a gradient descent algorithm. However, BP alone has several problems for deep networks. This section addresses the deep learning approach to handle the high dimensional data of the search space and thus the output is contrasted with random forest and logistic regression methods.

6.3.1 Deep belief network

Deep Belief network (DBN) is an unsupervised learning algorithm proposed by Hinton in 2006 for classifying deep generative models. A DBN consists of a series of Restricted Boltzmann Machinery (RBM). The kernel of the DBN is a rapacious, layer-by - layer classification algorithm that increases the intensity of DBN. Separately, the initialization of MLP weights with a similarly configured DBN always yields substantially better results than random weights.

As DBN is associated with Energy based models, so algorithm is explained below:

For a given RBM, Let's relate energy function with the units as,

$$Energy(m,n) = -a'n - b'm - n'Wm \quad (1)$$

Where p and q defines the offsets/ biases. W constitutes the weights linking components

The probability of p (visible) and q (hidden) units is:

$$P(m,n) = \frac{1}{Y} e^{-Energy(m,n)} \quad (2)$$

Where Y defines normalization term.

Let's calculate free energy form by marginalizing 'n'

$$P(m,n) = \frac{\Sigma n}{Y} e^{-Energy(m,n)} = \frac{e^{-FreeEnergy(m)}}{Y} \quad (3)$$

Using the free energy method enables the measurement of gradients easier.
Energy function can be re-written as:

$$Energy(m,n) = -\beta(m) - \Sigma_i \gamma_i(m, n_i) \quad (4)$$

Factorizing P(m) gives:

$$P(m,n) = \frac{\Sigma_n e^{-Energy(m,n)}}{Y} = \frac{e^{-FreeEnergy(m)}}{Y}$$

$$= \frac{1}{Y} \Sigma_{n_1} \Sigma_{n_2} \dots \Sigma_{n_k} e^{\beta(m) - \Sigma_i \gamma_i (m,n_i)}$$

$$= \frac{1}{Y} \Sigma_{n_1} \Sigma_{n_2} \dots \Sigma_{n_k} e^{\beta(m)} \prod_i e^{-\gamma_i}(m, ni)$$

$$= \frac{e^{\beta(m)}}{Y} \sum_{n_1} e^{-\gamma_1(m,n_1)} \sum_{n_2} e^{-\gamma_2(m,n_2)} \ldots \sum_{n_k} e^{-\gamma_k(m,n_k)}$$

$$= \frac{e^{\beta(m)}}{Y} \prod_i \sum_{n_k} e^{-\gamma_i(m,n_i)}$$

DBN is used for a wide range of topics, varying from Recognition of images to recommendation algorithms and modeling of different subjects.

6.3.2 Auto Encoders

Autoencoders are a type of Artificial Neural networks, falling in category of unsupervised learning technique that allows using neural network for representing learning tasks. It helps minimize the dimensionality of the data to reconstruct a supervised learning task which generates a representation as close as possible to its original input from the reduced encoding (Wang et al. 2016).

Autoencoder is defined as a network constituting a single hidden layer where the input and output layer are of similar size as depicted in figure 6.1 and is explained with the help of Algorithm 5. Assume that input w belongs to m dimensional space i.e. $w \in P^m$ and new representation in n dimensional space. Let us say hidden layer has x nodes. Consider weight matrix $M \in P^{m*n}$ and bias vector in V and V' in P^m and P^n respectively.

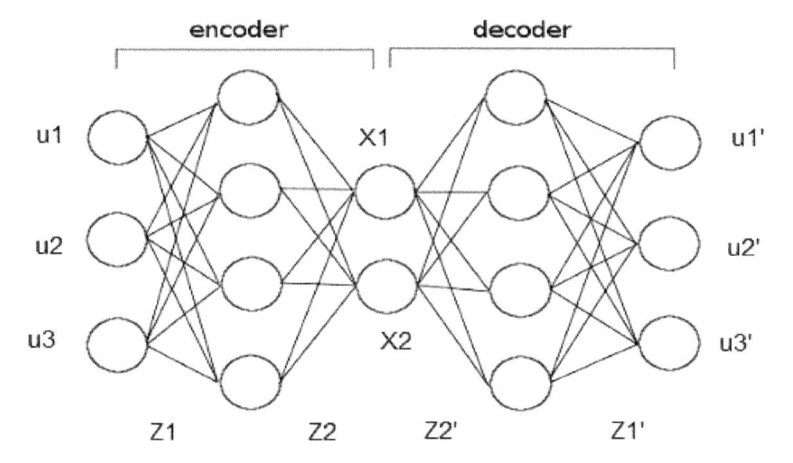

Figure 6.1: Layout of the Autocoder.

Let $s(w) = \frac{1}{1+e^{-w}}$ be logistic function. While using auto encoders for encoding the data, calculate the vector x= s(Mw + b). For decoding and framing the original input back, calculate y= s (M^{T}x + b').In decoding stage, the weight matrix is a transpose of a encoding stage to reduce the dimensionality of the data. To make the reconstruction as identical to the actual input, there is a need to optimise parameters like M, b, b' for certain loss function.

The Loss function is represented as:

$$E(z,y) = \frac{1}{2}(z-y)^2 \quad (5)$$

Where z is the original input. After the auto encoder is trained, the decoding step is rejected and the encoding step is considered as a preprocessing phase for transforming training inputs. Once the autoencoder is trained, it can be used to train the second autoencoder on the basis of the output received from the first autoencoder layer. By repeating these steps indefinitely, stacked autoencoders can be created. It has been observed that every successive trained layer assimilate an improved representation of the outer layer compared to the previous layers.

Derivative output error was calculated with reference to Matrix weight M_{ij} and computed gradient was used to define the hidden layers. Typically we need n < m for regular autoencoders such that Learned input representation occurs in lesser dimensional space than the input. This is performed to make sure that no trivial transformation of identity is learned by the autoencoder. A variant is other denoising auto encoders to learn representations using different reconstruction criteria (Vincent et al. 2008). Denoising helps autoencoder in understanding the real structure of input data and hence learns to conduct good representation. After an Autoencoder has been fully trained using denoising criteria, a deep autoencoder becomes an inventive model.

Algorithm 5: Algorithm for Auto Encoders

Step I:. Data is obtained and preprocessing is performed i.e cleaning of the data and import the required libraries

Step II: Build the neural network. Shape the data which can be read by neural network.

Step III: Convert data into Torch Tensors.

Step IV: Architecture of neural network is created

    Step IV i: Activation function is built

    Step IV ii: Calculate the probability of activated neurons

    Step IV iii: Weight and biases are updated.

Step V: Auto Encoder is trained.

    Step V i: Epochs were initialized

    Step V ii: Create batch for training

    Step V iii: Weight are updated.

Step V.1: Test the AutoEncoder

Step VII: Exit

6.4 EXPERIMENTAL SETUP FOR ONLINE BEHAVIOR OF CUSTOMERS

6.4.1 Data preprocessing

Each session is recorded with a unique time stamp Id corresponding to each activity. The users are directed to click on the products in that session. The click duration of the user can be calculated easily by subtracting the time of user's first click from the time of user's next click. To find how longer the product appears in the user's session, we calculate it by adding the time span of the clicks in which the product appears. The data is then sorted on the basis of timestamp ID and ItemDuration attribute is then appended to each clicked data. Then any other property which is specific to a product is also extracted and appended to clicked data as depicted in table 6.1. In addition, the Click-Buy ratio is determined by aggregating the click-Buy ratio across all items in a session.

We restricted the collection of 257 product categories to frame a dataset. Weekly aggregation of data was carried out on the basis of the product category. In order to predict sales with at least 1 day of lag, the addition to the cart event was not considered in the first step because it consisted of data prepared on the very same day / session of sales events. It was considered in second duration. The users whose clicks were less than 10 on a website were eliminated. Thus, the data thereby framed was balanced data consisting of an equal number of sales activities and non-sale activities. For predicting purchases within 24hour time, events were excluded in this time span. Table 5 describes six different datasets framed for testing the models. Buying session is represented with dimensions in the table. On all non-buying sessions, sub-sampling was performed to balance the datasets. Session id was used for sorting all click and buy sessions. Total number of sessions in the dataset was 45, 00,450 of which 152500 buy sessions were used for test data. The Click data for the buying session consists of a selection of items purchased, represented by Ds. For each i ∈ Ds, both session-based and product-based features were retrieved.

Table 6.2: Dataset framed for test models

Data	Dimension	Illustration
Dataset 1	2000	Weekly average sales data
Dataset 2	12000	Similar in features to dataset1 but consists of larger data size
Dataset 3	35000	Similar in features to dataset1 but consists of larger data size
Dataset 4	12000	Similar dataset 2 but is half weekly average
Dataset 5	12000	Similar to dataset 1 but with 1500 categories
Dataset 6	35000	Similar to dataset but with 1500 categories

6.4.2 Non-Negative matrix Approximation

Non-negative Matrix approximation (NMA), also known as Non-negative matrix factorization (NMF) is a feature extraction algorithm belonging to unsupervised learning class. NMA is a set of algorithms in Linear algebra and multivariate analysis where matrix M is factorized into (usually) two W and H matrixes, with the rule that all three matrixes have no negative elements. This non-negative feature makes it easier to inspect the matrices (Huang et al. 2012). We use this NMA method for reducing the high dimensionality in the data. Here dataset 5 is used to reduce the dimensionality using NMA method.

Given a non-negative matrix M, consisting of training data. NMA factorize the data into two matrixes mentioned above W and H, such that $M = \sim WH$

Let M ∈ Q^{a*b} and positive integer k < min (a, b),

Find non-negative matrix W∈Q^{a*k} and H∈Q^{k*b} to minimize

$$F(W,H) = \frac{1}{2} \|M-WH\|^2_F$$

The main objective of NMA is to reduce data to a subset of features. The value of k helps influence the results and assuming that k meets the criteria of k<min(a,b) as k represents the low rank of original matrix M.

6.4.3 Regularization

Regularization is a method which allows minor improvements to the learning algorithm, so that the model becomes more generalised. It thus improves the performance of the model even on the unseen results. It helps reduce the generalisation error even if the training error is increasing. It helps penalizes the weight matrices of the nodes as stated by Kang and Tao (2018).

Particularly the avoidance of over fitting is a crucial part for deep neural networks having parameters in billions or millions. DBN could create large and responsive models capable of describing diverse input / output dependencies. To train a larger network and to keep the bias and variance down at the same time is only possible with the help of Regularisation. To add more data to minimize the variance and without affecting the bias, it is necessary to conduct regularisation. There are many regularisation techniques like L1/L2, dropout, etc which help reduce the variance. In this paper, we opted for Dropout regularisation technique as L2 shifted the weight towards zero which is further not desirable. Dropout regularisation is the most important technique among all other regularization techniques. It randomly selects nodes at every iteration and removes it along with all input and output connections. It is much related to ensemble method in machine learning in which every iteration consists of separate set of nodes and also produces different set of outputs. Dropout marginalises heavy weights, leading to inaccurate predictions or activating hidden units. The value of 0.25 is defined as the probability of dropping as shown in figure 6.2.

```
model = Sequential([
Dense(output_dim=hidden1_num_units, input_dim=input_num_units, activation='relu'),
Dropout(0.25),

Dense(output_dim=output_num_units, input_dim=hidden5_num_units, activation='softmax'),
])
```

Figure 6.2: Dropout value of Regularization

The graphical representation of Epochs and the loss so occurred during the training process has been illustrated with the help of figure 6.3. Regularization technique helped in minimizing these losses.

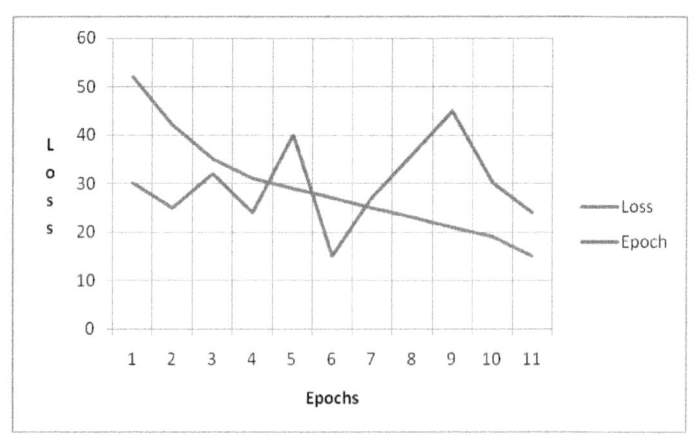

Figure 6.3: Denoising Autoencoder with Epochs and Loss

6.4.4 Optimization

Zhang, Z. (2018) defined Optimization as a technique that binds the loss function and parameter values together by updating the model according to the loss function output. In other words, by futzing with the weights, optimizers shape and mould the model to the most accurate possible form. The loss function is the terrain guide, which informs the optimizer whether it is going in the right or wrong direction. Optimization algorithms or techniques are critical for minimising losses and producing much possible reliable as results. We have used Adam optimiser as discussed below.

6.4.4a Adam optimizer:

Adam is an adaptive learning performance optimisation algorithm primarily designed to train deep neural networks [optimizer paper]. In this, individual learning rates are calculated for various parameters. It originates from adaptive moment estimation, and the reason it's labelled as Adam, is because Adam utilizes first and second order estimates to accommodate the learning rate for each neural network weight (Sun et al. 2020).

Let **μ(t) and σ(t)** be the Mean value and the uncentered variance of the gradients respectively. They are considered as different order of momentums and are represented as:

$$\mu_t' = \frac{\mu_t}{1-\beta_1^t}$$

$$\sigma_t' = \frac{\sigma_t}{1-\beta_2^t}$$

First and second order of momentum

Then a mean of μ(t) and σ(t) is calculated so that E(μ(t)) is equal to E(g(t)) and we get the updated parameter as:

$$\gamma_{t+1} = \gamma_t - \frac{\eta}{\sqrt{\sigma_t' + \epsilon}} \mu_t'$$

The values for β1 is 0.8 , 0.888 for β2, and (10 x exp(-8)) for 'ϵ'. The values for β1 is 0.8 , 0.888 for β2, and (10 x exp(-8)) for 'ϵ'. Reduced loss with the application of Adam optimizer is described below in figure 6.4.

```
Epoch 1/6
350/350 [==================] - 3s 10ms/step - loss:0.1254 - accuracy:0.9767 - val_loss:9.0114 - val_accuracy:0.127
Epoch 2/6
350/350 [==================] - 3s 9ms/step - loss:0.0879 - accuracy:0.9823 - val_loss:6.4251 - val_accuracy:0.2198
Epoch 3/6
350/350 [==================] - 3s 9ms/step - loss:0.0587 - accuracy:0.9923 - val_loss:0.4247 - val_accuracy:0.3211
Epoch 4/6
350/350 [==================] - 3s 9ms/step - loss:0.0284 - accuracy:0.9928 - val_loss:0.0.0991 - val_accuracy:0.95
Epoch 5/6
350/350 [==================] - 3s 9ms/step - loss:0.0220 - accuracy:0.9954 - val_loss:0.0.0628 - val_accuracy:0.98
Epoch 6/6
350/350 [==================] - 3s 9ms/step - loss:0.0145 - accuracy:0.9984 - val_loss:0.0.0502 - val_accuracy:0.98
Test Loss using Adam: 0.046814525783256225939 / Test accuracy: 0.9878999412569958
```

Figure 6.4: Adam Optimiser result

6.5 RESULTS

The proposed model is an effective method in predicting the online customer behaviour with the help of click streams. In this, Table 6.2 in section 6.4.1 is considered for executing the algorithms. Being a low dimensional data, Logistic regression and Random forest algorithms and ensemble method was applied. Most of the purchase events occurred within one day frame i.e. 24hours. AUC was calculated for Logistic regression, Random Forest Algorithm and Ensemble methods as 0.61, 0.64 and 0.66 respectively. Further Table 6.1 and Table 6.2 were combined to calculate AUC for different datasets and results are represented in graph in figure 6.5.

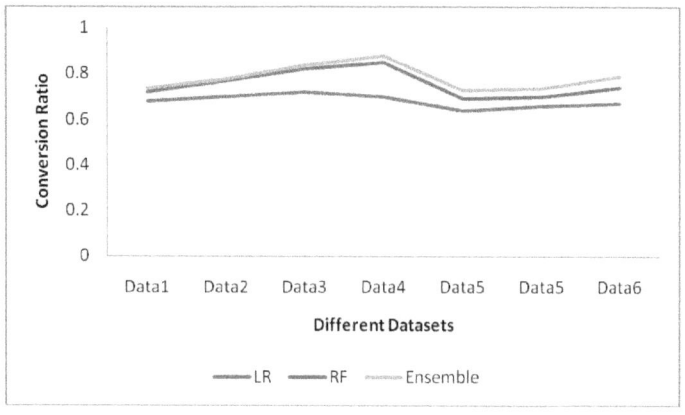

Figure 6.5: AUC Curve for Different Classifiers

In this sample size plays an important role in Algorithms' performance and from the above figure 6.3 Ensemble methods shows better performance than Random Forest then logistic Regression. Dataset 4 explains that the time of events is a significant factor to be considered despite of increasing the search space. Dataset 5 concludes only data with 300 features has improved the accuracy of the results and NMF did some data compression, but not in an optimal manner. So Auto encoders were applied to reduce the dimensionality of the data having product categories in thousands.

Further DBN results were analysed and the main benefits of using DBN is that it can consider all data irrespective of whether it is labelled or unlabeled for pre- training the data. DBN can capture a high-order association of visible data for pattern recognition, even if no information on targeted class labels is available. A total of around 2 million sessions is considered, i.e. page views of products measured in aggregation to each user and on per week basis with parameters described in Table 6.1. Training and testing data was prepared by dividing the data into ratio of 70:30. Training set was further segregated into 4 folds and each model was trained four times with these four folds to be considered as validation data. Average of four folds is considered for AUC in evaluating test sets. To select the best model among all the other models, performance parameters were evaluated on validation data. Metaparameter tuning was provided by hand to the baseline models.

There are several other metaparameters in neural networks, including optimization, such as learning levels and momentum values; architectural, such as layer sizes and hidden units; and regularisation, such as dropout likelihood for each layer. In this model, all neural metaparameters were setup using the Adam Optimizer to optimize the AUC validation. The benefit of using Adam optimization algorithm is that it requires less memory, is computationally efficient for noisy functions and is well suited to the dataset having larger parameters or data. Adam was used to optimise the metaparameters. Table 6.3 depicts the metaparameters considered and different set was chosen, based on the iteration of a single hidden layer to train the model.

Table 6.3: Metaparameters considered for training the dataset

Metaparameters	Values
Training Epochs	∈ [10:200] for single hidden layer ∈ [10:250] for 2 or above hidden layers
Count of hidden elements in each Layer	• No hidden layer up to 500 units • 16 hidden units for single task neural network • 64 for all others
Dropout function	∈ [0 : 0.25]
Delay fraction	∈ [0: 1] The proportion of training iterations that must be completed before the start of the learning level.
Average gradient's Initial Learning Rate	∈ [0.001 : 0.20]
Momentum	∈ [0 : 0.97]
L2 weight cost	∈ [0: 0.01]
SDA : Noise level applied to Input layer	∈ [0:0.1]

Dataset 3 having 35000 purchase transactions was used for optimizing the parameters on the network and same parameters were used on other datasets. It was observed that Dropout for Rectified Linear unit (ReLU) networks was always maintained; while it sigmoid transfer function it hardly was greater than zero. The graph in the figure 6.6 represents the page view events for different subsets of the data.

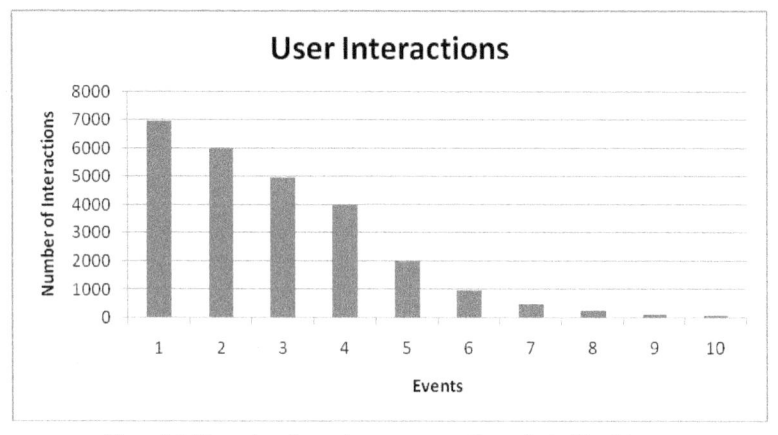

Figure 6.6: Dispersion of pageview occurrences for a subset of the data.

The training model trained with Autoencoders and optimizers generated better results and reached the highest accuracy as depicted in the Figure 6.7

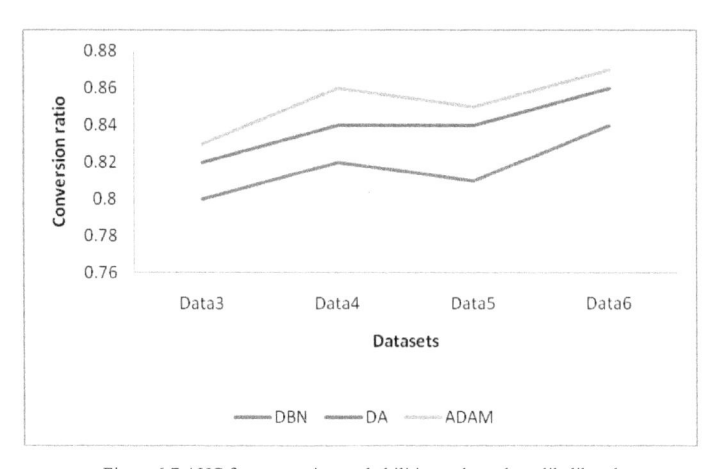

Figure 6.7 AUC for conversion probabilities and purchase likelihood

CHAPTER 7
DEVELOPING A VIRTUAL ASSISTANT IN RESPOND TO BUSINESS SERVICES

7.1 INTRODUCTION

Chatbots are of great benefit to business entities and even to consumers. Most people prefer chatting directly from a chatbox rather than calling service centres. The way people handle customer care has changed with the social media. Almost half of the U.S. Internet users turn to social media for help as they can easily submit a Tweet or Facebook status instead of calling any number or writing a detailed email (Nielsen 2011). Twitter users send billions of requests to major brands every month. With the exponential increase in the amount of user requests, processing and addressing incoming requests has become increasingly difficult. Many organizations are creating dedicated customer service teams to resolve this issue and respond to different requests on social media. The team consists of dozens or hundreds of human users trained to meet the needs of target users (Murray 1991). However, addressing manually all the queries is not possible and somehow fails to fulfill user's expectations. Studies have found that 75 per cent of users who have ever question a Twitter brand expect an answer within an hour (Xu et al. 2017). Yet our analysis of millions of data shows that the average response time is 6.5 hours. This gap has led to the development of chatbots.

Chatbot identifies the user input, and access information to provide a predefined acknowledgement by using pattern matching. For example, if the user gives the bot a sentence such as, "What is your name?"Most likely the chatbot will respond something like" My name is Chatbot, "or the chatbot will reply as" You can call me Chatbot, "depending on the user's sentence (Dahiya 2017)

7.2 IMPLEMENTATION PROCESS

Chatbot is a computer programme that mimics human communication using artificial intelligence. It helps the consumer responding to the questions they have asked. Now a day's many tools and techniques are available for developing chatbots. Detailed Implementation of a chatbot is discussed below:

To implement a chatbot, RASA is used, a library associated to deep learning along with natural language processing toolkit(NLTK) and other useful libraries.

Step 1: Import Libraries & Load the Data

A python file named "train_chatbot" was created and then all the necessary modules were imported. After that, the JSON data file in our Python programme will be read.

Requirements:
python = 3.6

python libraries:
pip install rasa-nlu==0.15.1
pip install sklearn
pip install sklearn_crfsuite
pip install rasa[spacy]
python -m spacy download en_core_web_md
python -m spacy link en_core_web_md en

Import libraries:
engin.py
import nltk.corpus
import nltk.tokenize.punkt
import nltk.stem.snowball
import string
from nltk.corpus import wordnet
from nltk.tokenize import WordPunctTokenizer
import numpy as np

from flask import Flask
from flask import render_template,jsonify,request
import requests
 # from models import *
from engine import *
import random
import pandas as pd
sentences=df[df.columns[1:]].apply(lambda x: ' '.join(x.dropna().astype(str)),axis=1).tolist()

#importing module
import logging

Here's a quick breakdown of the components:

- **engin.py** — *the code for reading in the product and brandin data into a training set and using a RASA and NLTK we have built intent and entity search functions which train our RASA model.*

- **api.py** — *the code for requentist response from interface, finding out intent and entities and creating a graphical interface for interacting with the chatbot etc........*

Step 2: Creating and Preprocessing the Data

To form a model, machine cannot take the raw data. For machine to understand it easily, lot of pre-processing is required. Tokenization and lemmatization is done by RASA itself in its library. Here we have 3 datasets:

1. data_base_final.csv : This dataset is manually created which has following columns: Brand, ProductName, ProductUPC, source of Information Here, source of Information is: links of ecommerce sites products (ex. Amazon, etc)
2. brand.txt : It has a list of all brands which is available: olay ,dove, lipton, knorr, axe, pampers, aveeno, neutrogena, colgate, tide, loreal, galt, brio, grafix, coca cola, summer infant, tippitoes.
3. productname.txt : It has a list of products just like brands.

Step 3: Create Training Model

Each input pattern is transformed into numbers to train the model. First, we're going to lemmatize each pattern word and create a list of zeroes of about the same length as that of total number of terms. Only those indexes that include the word in the patterns will be set to value 1. Similarly, by applying 1 to the input class to which the pattern belongs, we set the output. Then we will convert a few examples of brand names and product names in the lookup table along with intents. This is where we insert our lookup table of brand names.

Note: some of the lookup table elements must be present in the training data(data_base_final.csv) for this to be effective.

Example:
lookup:brand
data/brand.txt

lookup:product
data/productname.txt

intent:brand_search
- i'm looking for a [colgate](brand) [toothpaste](product)
- i am looking for [olay](brand) [regenerist](product)
- I want to buy [dove](brand) [soap](product)

intent:offers_search
- show offers on [dettol](brand)
- offers on [colgate](brand)
- Any offers on [colgate](brand) [optic white toothpaste](product)

intent:greet
- hey
- hello
- hello there
- good morning

Here we also need to create random responses for the greet messages:

Example:

If user asks questions to our bot like:

1. hey ---> Response: "How can I help you?"

2. Hi ---> Response: "Ask me a question regarding the products or brands you are looking for."

Here we built a function where chatbot will respond random answers with the help of following logic depicted in figure 7.1 and figure 7.2:

get_random_response = lambda intent:random.choice(intent_response_dict[intent])

```python
get_random_response = lambda intent:random.choice(intent_response_dict[intent])
app.logger.debug('Starting..............................\n')
@app.route('/chat',methods=["POST"])
def chat():
    try:
        user_message = request.form["text"]
        app.logger.debug('user_message -:{}'.format(user_message))
        response = requests.get("http://localhost:5000/parse",params={"q":user_message})
        response = response.json()
        entities = response.get("entities")
        topresponse = response["topScoringIntent"]
        intent = topresponse.get("intent")
        print("Intent {}, Entities {}".format(intent,entities))
        if intent == "brand_search":
            response_text = brand_search(entities,sentences)# "Sorry will get answer soon"
        elif intent == "offers_search":
            response_text = offers_search(entities,sentences)
        else:
            response_text = [get_random_response(intent)]
        # logging.info("bot_message : {}".format(response_text))
        app.logger.debug('bot_message -:{}'.format(response_text))
        return jsonify({"status":"success","response":response_text})
    except Exception as e:
        print(e)
        return jsonify({"status":"success","response":["Sorry I am not trained to do that y
```

Figure 7.1: Logic Implementation in chatbot to respond to random answers

```
##dict of response for each type of intent
intent_response_dict = {
    "intro": ["Ask me a question regarding the products or brands you are looking for."],
    "greet":["Ask me a question regarding the products or brands you are looking for.","Hey,How can I help you?","Hi,How can I help you?","Hello, How can I help you?"],
    "goodbye":["Bye","It was nice talking to you","See you"],
    "affirm":["Cool","I know you would like it"],
    "thankyou":["Thank you"," You're welcome!"]

}

intent_response_dict_tel = {
    "intro": ["hi {}, Ask me a question regarding the products or brands you are looking for."],
    "greet":["who are you? {}, Ask me a question regarding the products or brands you are looking for.","Hey {}, How can I help you?","Hi {}, How can I help you?","Hello {}, How can I help you?"],
    "goodbye":["Bye {}","It was nice talking to you {}","See you {}"],
    "affirm":["Cool {}","{} I know you would like it"],
    "thankyou":["Thank you {}","You're welcome!{}"]
```

Figure 7.2: Dictionary of intro, greet and end intents

Step 4. Train the Model

The architecture of our model would be a neural network comprised of three dense layers. The first layer contains 128 neurons, the middle has 64, and then the last layer has the same neurons as that of the number of classes. Drop-out layers are added to reduce the overfit of the model. We used the SGD optimiser and data was chip in to start training the model. Below commands are performed to train the model on any machine.

Training

python -m rasa_nlu.train -c config.json -d data/product_train_lookup.md
After training rasa_nlu pretrained models will dump in
models/nlu/default/model_[time]
here [time] will be a number when we complete training.

Step 5: Interacting with your chatbot

For the model to chat, a graphical User interface is created for it to interact and is named as gui chatbot.py. In this model, rasa_nlu is used and it is necessary to keep running rasa server and app.py (our flask API) with the following commands mentioned below and depicted in the figure 7.3.

Structure of the desktop application is built in GUI file and the user messages are captured and some preprocessing is performed again before inputting the message into our trained model. User's message is then predicted in our model, and responses are selected randomly from the response list available in the intents file.

Server

python -m rasa_nlu.server -c config.json -e luis --path models/nlu

python app.py

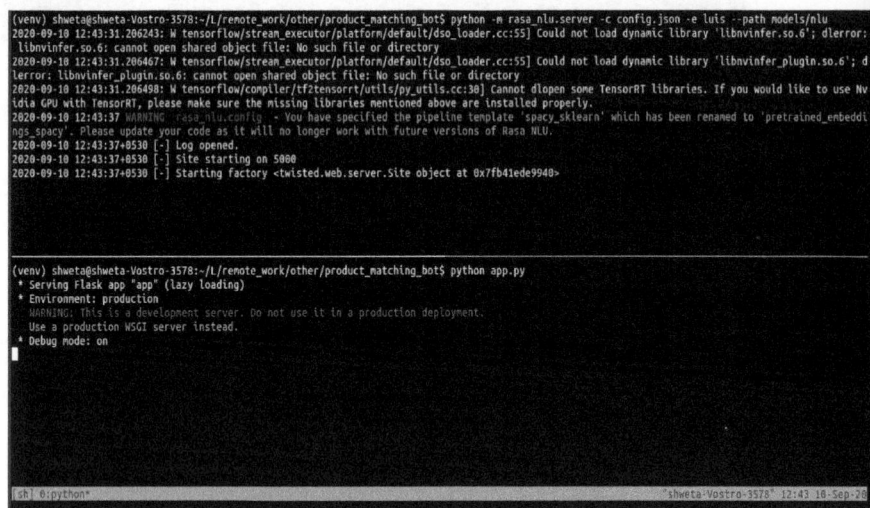

Figure 7.3: Running server and configuring the system

Step 6. Running the Chatbot

This is a web based chatbot with UI capabilities like: html, css, javascript. To access the Chatbot we need to run following command in google chrome browser:

http://localhost:8080/

7.3 RESULTS

GUI based results are shown in figure 7.4 and 7.5

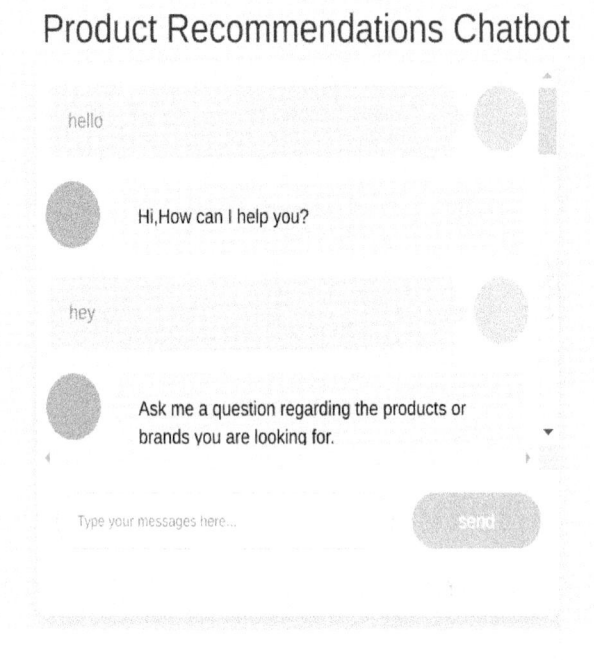

Figure 7.4: GUI based Chatbot interaction

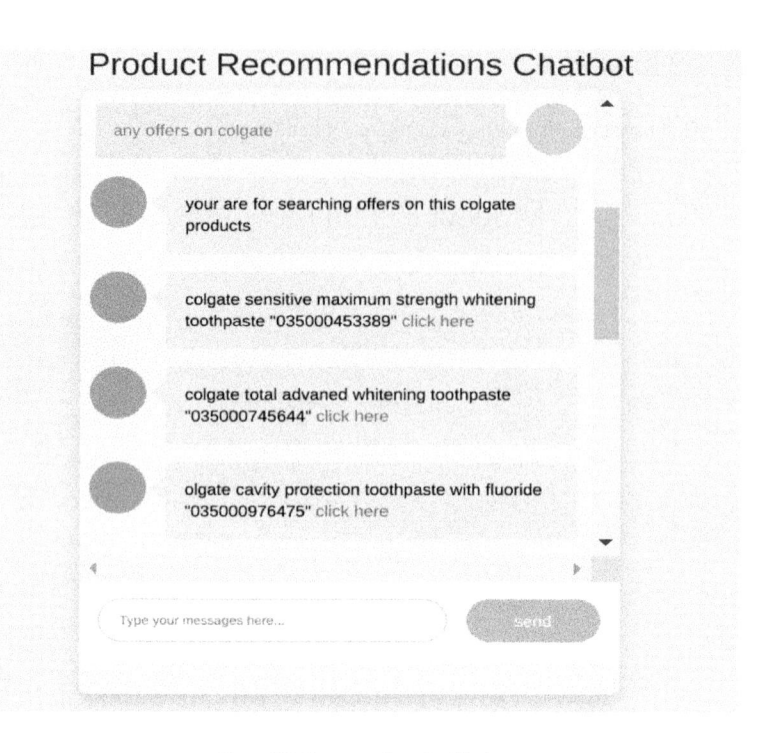

Figure 7.5: Response from the Chatbot

CHAPTER 8: CONCLUSION & FUTURE SCOPE

In E-Commerce Calculating similarity between goods in various domains is still a daunting area of research in e-commerce. Debilitating user's preferences and understanding their choice and behavior is one of the crucial matters for all e-commerce agencies. With the proliferation in IT field, it has become viable to understand and interpret the customer's need in the most advantageous and efficacious way. In this paper, a proposed system is used for finding users with similar preferences and recommending products using data analytics. User-item and Cosine Similarity are two main elements for finding similar users among lakhs of dataset. Artificial intelligence in CRM is utilized for analysis of information effectively and sharing it with other users. Chapter 4 laid emphasis on finding similarity of the users with the previous purchased products and check for the response time, Root mean square error and precision rate in contrast to already existing other similarity algorithm. More precisely, a buyer's list and viewer's list is prepared to generate purchase count and user-item matrix which are then formulated to find similarity and provide them recommendations to each user. The proposed model is compared with baseline similarity recommendations algorithms i.e popularity based model. Implementation of the Proposed System provides better results with less error rate and high response time. In Chapter 5, the proposed system was developed using the effective techniques of data mining, machine learning and statistical methods to predict purchases. This framework has been evaluated for an e-commerce firm on a broad dataset, and findings are promising enough to fully incorporate the system. The model has been evaluated against the ROC curve and Random forest method gives better results in comparison to logistic regression method. Various industries operating in online mode, the general framework can be applied and can be tailored to specific applications. This research can be further expanded depending on the attributes to be selected as per their requirements. In Chapter 6 online user behaviour of the customer was studied. Machine learning methods, including deep neural networks, have been used for modelling user behaviour and predicting purchases. We showed that a random forest and Ensemble method boosts the performance over linear model like logistic regression. Deep belief networks, auto encoders and ADAM optimisers were applied to model the user behaviour including clicks, sessions maintained and the user conversions. Different approaches were implemented to derive user behaviour from Clickstream data. Implementing Deep noising autoencoders and Adam optimisers has improved a result and gives us the accurate user conversions on the basis of different datasets so framed. This task is relevant for Digital Marketing and E-commerce Websites. Empirical results revealed that ensemble classifier predicts user conversions more accurately in combination to deep learning methods. Further analysis can involve real-time data testing, and effects on real time data. If model is fine tuned a bit to make it as a discriminative model, it can further be used to parallel train multiple networks and the output can be fed to a matrix individually. Chapter 7 discusses about product recommendation Chabot based on keywords on products. Here we can ask Chabot about your products which we're looking for. For examples: Body wash, toothpaste, shampoo, face cream, tea bags. Here not only products we can search multiple products of a single brand. Fox ex. Dove brand products: body wash, shampoo, bathing bar, deodorant, face cream and lot more. It helps to provide the recommendation for the specific products we are looking for. This model has been trained with limited products and brands and can further be extended to train more products.

REFERENCES

1. Abdi, F., & Abolmakarem, S. (2018). Customer Behavior Mining Framework (CBMF) using clustering and classification techniques. *Journal of Industrial Engineering International*, *15*(S1), 1–18. https://doi.org/10.1007/s40092-018-0285-3
2. Adair, B. (2018). *CRM Features List: CRM Functionality & Capabilities Checklist*. SelectHub raquo. https://www.selecthub.com/customer-relationship-management/crm-features-functionality-list/
3. Ali, M., & Lee, Y. (2018). CRM Sales Prediction Using Continuous Time-Evolving Classification. *AAAI*.
4. Amroush, F., Yusuf, T., & Baderddeen, A. (2010). *Using Artificial intelligence to select the optimal E-CRM ...* https://mpra.ub.uni-muenchen.de/25758/1/MPRA_paper_25758.pdf.
5. *Artificial Intelligence (AI) in CRM: It's not Skynet. Yet*. NexJ Systems Inc. (2017, February 13). http://www.nexj.com/2017/08/02/artificial-intelligence-ai-in-crm-its-not-skynet-yet.
6. Arunachalam, D., & Kumar, N. (2018). Benefit-based consumer segmentation and performance evaluation of clustering approaches: An evidence of data-driven decision-making. *Expert Systems with Applications*, *111*, 11–34. https://doi.org/10.1016/j.eswa.2018.03.007
7. Aslam, S., & Ashraf, I. (2014, July). *Data Mining Algorithms and their applications in Education Data Mining*. ResearchGate. https://www.researchgate.net/publication/266870775_Data_Mining_Algorithms_and_their_applications_in_Education_Data_Mining.
8. Baecke, P., & Poel, D. V. D. (2012). Including spatial interdependence in customer acquisition models: A cross-category comparison. *Expert Systems with Applications*, *39*(15), 12105–12113. https://doi.org/10.1016/j.eswa.2012.04.008
9. Baker, K. (2019). *12 Key Benefits CRM Systems Provide to a Business*. HubSpot Blog. https://blog.hubspot.com/sales/benefits-of-crm.
10. Bali, J., & Nayak, S. (2020). Artificial Intelligence. *Journal of Clinical Ophthalmology and Research*, *8*(1), 1. https://doi.org/10.4103/jcor.jcor_18_20
11. Balonin, N. A., Petoukhov, S. V., & Sergeev, M. B. (2017). Matrices in Improvement of Systems of Artificial Intelligence and Education of Specialists. *Advances in Intelligent Systems and Computing Advances in Artificial Systems for Medicine and Education*, 39–52. https://doi.org/10.1007/978-3-319-67349-3_4

12. Barragáns-Martínez, B., Costa-Montenegro, E., & Juncal-Martínez, J. (2015). Developing a recommender system in a consumer electronic device. *Expert Systems with Applications*, *42*(9), 4216–4228. https://doi.org/10.1016/j.eswa.2015.01.052
13. Batista, L., Dibb, S., Meadows, M., Hinton, M., & Analogbei, M. (2018). A CRM-based pathway to improving organisational responsiveness: an empirical study. *Journal of Strategic Marketing*, *28*(6), 494–521. https://doi.org/10.1080/0965254x.2018.1555547
14. Belarbi, H., Tajmouati, A., Bennis, H., & Mohammed, E. H. T. (2016, November). *Predictive Analysis of Big Data in Retail Industry*. https://www.researchgate.net/profile/Hamid_Bennis/publication/311900279_Predictive_Analysis_of_Big_Data_in_Retail_Industry/links/5860609308ae329d61fadc4b/Predictive-Analysis-of-Big-Data-in-Retail-Industry.pdf.
15. Bhagat, R., Muralidharan, S., Lobzhanidze, A., & Vishwanath, S. (2018). Buy It Again. *Proceedings of the 24th ACM SIGKDD International Conference on Knowledge Discovery & Data Mining*. https://doi.org/10.1145/3219819.3219891
16. Bhandari, A., Gupta, A., & Das, D. (2015). Improvised Apriori Algorithm Using Frequent Pattern Tree for Real Time Applications in Data Mining. *Procedia Computer Science*, *46*, 644–651. https://doi.org/10.1016/j.procs.2015.02.115
17. Bhatia, B. S. (2008). *Management of service sector*. Deep & Deep Publications.
18. Bhosale,S., Salunkhe, A., Sutar,S. (2020, March) ARTIFICIAL INTELLIGENCE AND ITS APPLICATIONS, *International Journal of Advance and Innovative Research*, Volume 7, Issue 1(VI):January-March, 2020 Part-1, ISSN 2394-7780
19. Bloguser. (2017, September 8). *History and Evolution of CRM Software*. VIENNA Advantage. https://viennaadvantage.com/blog/technologies/history-of-crm-software/.
20. Bobadilla, J., Serradilla, F., & Hernando, A. (2009). Collaborative filtering adapted to recommender systems of e-learning. *Knowledge-Based Systems*, *22*(4), 261–265. https://doi.org/10.1016/j.knosys.2009.01.008
21. Bonanno, S. (2019, October 18). *10 CRM Features and Why You Need Them*. Software Buying Tips and Advice for Businesses. https://blog.capterra.com/12-crm-features-and-why-you-need-them/.
22. Borge, N.,(2016, June) Artificial Intelligence to improve education/Learning challenges. *International Journal of Advanced Engineering & Innovative Technology (IJAEIT)* ISSN: 2348 7208

23. Bradlow, E. T., Gangwar, M., Kopalle, P., & Voleti, S. (2017). The Role of Big Data and Predictive Analytics in Retailing. *Journal of Retailing*, *93*(1), 79–95. https://doi.org/10.1016/j.jretai.2016.12.004
24. Bressan, M., Leucci, S., Panconesi, A., Raghavan, P., & Terolli, E. (2016). The Limits of Popularity-Based Recommendations, and the Role of Social Ties. *Proceedings of the 22nd ACM SIGKDD International Conference on Knowledge Discovery and Data Mining*. https://doi.org/10.1145/2939672.2939797
25. Brito, P. Q., Soares, C., Almeida, S., Monte, A., & Byvoet, M. (2015). Customer segmentation in a large database of an online customized fashion business. *Robotics and Computer-Integrated Manufacturing*, *36*, 93–100. https://doi.org/10.1016/j.rcim.2014.12.014
26. Carnein, M., & Trautmann, H. (2019). Customer Segmentation Based on Transactional Data Using Stream Clustering. *Advances in Knowledge Discovery and Data Mining Lecture Notes in Computer Science*, 280–292. https://doi.org/10.1007/978-3-030-16148-4_22
27. Chagas, B. N. R., Viana, J. A. N., Reinhold, O., Lobato, F., Jacob, A. F. L., & Alt, R. (2018). Current Applications of Machine Learning Techniques in CRM: A Literature Review and Practical Implications. *2018 IEEE/WIC/ACM International Conference on Web Intelligence (WI)*. https://doi.org/10.1109/wi.2018.00-53
28. Charoensukmongkol, P., & Sasatanun, P. (2017). Social media use for CRM and business performance satisfaction: The moderating roles of social skills and social media sales intensity. *Asia Pacific Management Review*, *22*(1), 25–34. https://doi.org/10.1016/j.apmrv.2016.10.005
29. Christy, A. J., Umamakeswari, A., Priyatharsini, L., & Neyaa, A. (2018). RFM ranking – An effective approach to customer segmentation. *Journal of King Saud University - Computer and Information Sciences*. doi:10.1016/j.jksuci.2018.09.004
30. CRM, S. (2016). AI for CRM: A Field Guide to Everything You Need to Know.
31. Curme, C., Preis, T., Stanley, H. E., & Moat, H. S. (2014). Quantifying the semantics of search behavior before stock market moves. *Proceedings of the National Academy of Sciences*, *111*(32), 11600–11605. https://doi.org/10.1073/pnas.1324054111
32. Dahiya, M. (2017, May). *A Tool of Conversation: Chatbot - ResearchGate*. https://www.researchgate.net/profile/Menal_Dahiya/publication/321864990_A_Tool_of_Conversation_Chatbot/links/5a360b02aca27247eddea031/A-Tool-of-Conversation-Chatbot.pdf.

33. Davenport, T., Guha, A., Grewal, D., & Bressgott, T. (2019). How artificial intelligence will change the future of marketing. *Journal of the Academy of Marketing Science, 48*(1), 24–42. https://doi.org/10.1007/s11747-019-00696-0
34. D'Haen, J., Poel, D. V. D., & Thorleuchter, D. (2013). Predicting customer profitability during acquisition: Finding the optimal combination of data source and data mining technique. *Expert Systems with Applications, 40*(6), 2007–2012. https://doi.org/10.1016/j.eswa.2012.10.023
35. Dhimas, D. (2012). Predictive Analytics. *Medical News , The Business of healthcare.* http://www.medicalnews.md/predictive-analytics/
36. Frankenfield, J. (2020, January 7). *How Artificial Intelligence Works.* Investopedia. https://www.investopedia.com/terms/a/artificial-intelligence-ai.asp.
37. Galloway, Chris, and Lukasz Swiatek. "Public Relations and Artificial Intelligence: It's Not (Just) about Robots." *Public Relations Review*, vol. 44, no. 5, 2018, pp. 734–740., doi:10.1016/j.pubrev.2018.10.008
38. Gavalas, D., Konstantopoulos, C., Mastakas, K., & Pantziou, G. (2014). Mobile recommender systems in tourism. *Journal of Network and Computer Applications, 39*, 319–333. https://doi.org/10.1016/j.jnca.2013.04.006
39. Geisel, A. (2018). The Current And Future Impact Of Artificial Intelligence On Business. *International Journal of Scientific & Technology Research, 7*, 116-122.
40. Gončarovs, P. (2017). Data Analytics in CRM Processes: A Literature Review. *Information Technology and Management Science, 20*(1). https://doi.org/10.1515/itms-2017-0018
41. Gordini, N., & Veglio, V. (2014). *Customer relationship management and data mining: A ...* https://www.researchgate.net/profile/Niccolo_Gordini/publication/259740867_Customer_Relationship_Management_and_Data_Mining_A_Classification_Decision_Tree_to_Predict_Customer_Purchasing_Behavior_in_Global_Market/links/560124e308aeba1d9f84ee43.pdf.
42. Guo, F., & Qin, H. (2017). Data Mining Techniques for Customer Relationship Management. *Journal of Physics: Conference Series, 910*, 012021. https://doi.org/10.1088/1742-6596/910/1/012021
43. Gupta, R., & Pathak, C. (2014). A Machine Learning Framework for Predicting Purchase by Online Customers based on Dynamic Pricing. *Procedia Computer Science, 36*, 599–605. https://doi.org/10.1016/j.procs.2014.09.06

44. Habul, A., & Pilav-Veli, A. (2012). Customer Relationship Management and Business Intelligence. *Advances in Customer Relationship Management.* https://doi.org/10.5772/30551
45. He, H., Zhang, W., & Zhang, S. (2018). A novel ensemble method for credit scoring: Adaption of different imbalance ratios. *Expert Systems with Applications*, *98*, 105–117. https://doi.org/10.1016/j.eswa.2018.01.012
46. Hinton, G. E. (2006). Reducing the Dimensionality of Data with Neural Networks. *Science, 313*(5786), 504-507. doi:10.1126/science.1127647
47. Holý, V., Sokol, O., & Černý, M. (2017). Clustering retail products based on customer behaviour. *Applied Soft Computing*, *60*, 752–762. https://doi.org/10.1016/j.asoc.2017.02.004
48. Hopkinsona, P., Vegab.P.R., and Singhala, A.,(2018) Exploring the use of AI to manage customers' relationships – Academic of marketing, workshop paper, *Artificial Intelligence in Marketing – The field, research directions, and methodological issues.*
49. Huang, Z., Zhou, A., & Zhang, G. (2012). Non-negative Matrix Factorization: A Short Survey on Methods and Applications. *Communications in Computer and Information Science Computational Intelligence and Intelligent Systems*, 331–340. https://doi.org/10.1007/978-3-642-34289-9_37
50. Hussain, Q. (2014). Getting the Most from CRM Systems: Data Mining in SugarCRM, Finding Important Patterns. *Human-Computer Interaction. Applications and Services Lecture Notes in Computer Science*, 693–699. https://doi.org/10.1007/978-3-319-07227-2_66
51. In, B. (2016). What is Artificial Intelligence? How Does AI Work?: Built In. What is Artificial Intelligence? How Does AI Work? | Built In. https://builtin.com/artificial-intelligence
52. Joshi, N. (2019, June 26). *7 Types Of Artificial Intelligence*. Forbes. https://www.forbes.com/sites/cognitiveworld/2019/06/19/7-types-of-artificial-intelligence/.
53. Kang, G., Li, J., & Tao, D. (2018). Shakeout: A New Approach to Regularized Deep Neural Network Training. *IEEE Transactions on Pattern Analysis and Machine Intelligence*, *40*(5), 1245–1258. https://doi.org/10.1109/tpami.2017.2701831
54. Khalili-Damghani, K., Abdi, F., & Abolmakarem, S. (2018). Hybrid soft computing approach based on clustering, rule mining, and decision tree analysis for customer segmentation problem: Real case of customer-centric industries. *Applied Soft Computing*, *73*, 816–828. https://doi.org/10.1016/j.asoc.2018.09.001

55. Khajvand, M., Zolfaghar, K., Ashoori, S., & Alizadeh, S. (2011). Estimating customer lifetime value based on RFM analysis of customer purchase behavior: Case study. *Procedia Computer Science, 3*, 57–63. https://doi.org/10.1016/j.procs.2010.12.011
56. Kiarashinejad, Y., Abdollahramezani, S., & Adibi, A. (2020). Deep learning approach based on dimensionality reduction for designing electromagnetic nanostructures. *Npj Computational Materials, 6*(1). https://doi.org/10.1038/s41524-020-0276-y
57. Kumar, V., Rajan, B., Venkatesan, R., & Lecinski, J. (2019). Understanding the Role of Artificial Intelligence in Personalized Engagement Marketing. *California Management Review, 61*(4), 135–155. https://doi.org/10.1177/0008125619859317
58. Kwong, C., Jiang, H., & Luo, X. (2016). AI-based methodology of integrating affective design, engineering, and marketing for defining design specifications of new products. *Engineering Applications of Artificial Intelligence, 47*, 49–60. https://doi.org/10.1016/j.engappai.2015.04.001
59. Lahitani, A. R., Permanasari, A. E., & Setiawan, N. A. (2016). Cosine similarity to determine similarity measure: Study case in online essay assessment. *2016 4th International Conference on Cyber and IT Service Management.* https://doi.org/10.1109/citsm.2016.7577578
60. Lemaignan, S., Warnier, M., Sisbot, E. A., Clodic, A., & Alami, R. (2017). Artificial cognition for social human–robot interaction: An implementation. *Artificial Intelligence, 247*, 45–69. https://doi.org/10.1016/j.artint.2016.07.002
61. Lepenioti, K., Bousdekis, A., Apostolou, D., & Mentzas, G. (2020). Prescriptive analytics: Literature review and research challenges. *International Journal of Information Management, 50*, 57–70. https://doi.org/10.1016/j.ijinfomgt.2019.04.003
62. Low, J. *Which Industries Are Investing In AI - And For What Purposes?* Down. http://www.thelowdownblog.com/2018/12/which-industries-are-investing-in-ai.html
63. Mahmoud, F. (2017, May). The Application of Predictive Analytics:Benefits,Challenges and How it can be improved. *International Journal of Scientific and Research Publications(vol 7) Issue5*, ISSN 2250-3153
64. Manigandan, E., Shanthi, V., & Kasthuri, M. (2018). Parallel Clustering for Data Mining in CRM. *Data Management, Analytics and Innovation Advances in Intelligent Systems and Computing*, 117–127. https://doi.org/10.1007/978-981-13-1402-5_9
65. Matty, C. (2017, February 2). *Artificial Intelligence Is the Next Step in CRM's Evolution.* CRM Magazine. http://www.destinationcrm.com/Articles/Web-

Exclusives/Viewpoints/Artificial-Intelligence-Is-the-Next-Step-in-CRMs-Evolution--116145.aspx?platform=hootsuite

66. Mekkamol, P., Piewdang, S., & Untachai, S. (2013). Modeling e-CRM for Community Tourism in Upper Northeastern Thailand. *Procedia - Social and Behavioral Sciences, 88*, 108–117. https://doi.org/10.1016/j.sbspro.2013.08.486

67. Meng, S., Dou, W., Zhang, X., & Chen, J. (2014). KASR: A Keyword-Aware Service Recommendation Method on MapReduce for Big Data Applications. *IEEE Transactions on Parallel and Distributed Systems, 25*(12), 3221–3231. https://doi.org/10.1109/tpds.2013.2297117

68. Mills, M. (2018). *How Artificial Intelligence Impacts Business Management*. Datafloq. https://datafloq.com/read/artificial-intelligence-impact-business-management/5244#!

69. Mirzaei, T., & Iyer, L. (2014). Application Of Predictive Analytics In Customer Relationship Management: A Literature Review And Classification

70. Mohanty, A., & Ranjana. (2019). Usage of Predictive Research on further Business. *International Journal of Innovative Technology and Exploring Engineering Regular Issue, 8*(11), 3464–3466. https://doi.org/10.35940/ijitee.k2559.0981119

71. Mukonyezi,I. (2015, December). Mining Social Media for predictive Analytics. https://www.researchgate.net/publication/307108047.

72. Murray, K. B. (1991). A Test of Services Marketing Theory: Consumer Information Acquisition Activities. *Journal of Marketing, 55*(1), 10. https://doi.org/10.2307/1252200

73. Ngai, E., Xiu, L., & Chau, D. (2009). Application of data mining techniques in customer relationship management: A literature review and classification. *Expert Systems with Applications, 36*(2), 2592–2602. https://doi.org/10.1016/j.eswa.2008.02.021

74. Nguyen, L. and A. Amer, A.,(2019). Advanced Cosine Measures for Collaborative Filtering, *Adaptation and Personalization Journal*, 1, pp21-41.

75. Nielsen. (2011, November 9). *State of the Media: Social Media Report Q3*. Nielsen. https://www.nielsen.com/us/en/insights/report/2011/social-media-report-q3/.

76. Osman, C.-C., & Ghiran, A.-M. (2019). Extracting Customer Traces from CRMS: From Software to Process Models. *Procedia Manufacturing, 32*, 619–626. https://doi.org/10.1016/j.promfg.2019.02.261

77. Pannu,A(2015, April 10) Artificial Intelligence and its applications. *International Journal of Engineering and Innovative Technology (IJEIT)*, Vol 4, Issue 10

78. Pereira, F. S. F., Gama, J., Amo, S. D., & Oliveira, G. M. B. (2018). On analyzing user preference dynamics with temporal social networks. *Machine Learning, 107*(11), 1745–1773. https://doi.org/10.1007/s10994-018-5740-2.
79. Point, J. T. (2015). *Types of Artificial Intelligence - Javatpoint*. www.javatpoint.com. https://www.javatpoint.com/types-of-artificial-intelligence.
80. Rao, V. S. H., & Kumar, M. N. (2012). A New Intelligence-Based Approach for Computer-Aided Diagnosis of Dengue Fever. *IEEE Transactions on Information Technology in Biomedicine, 16*(1), 112–118. https://doi.org/10.1109/titb.2011.2171978
81. Rivas, G. (2020, June 24). *AI and CRM: Enhance Customer Relationship through Artificial Intelligence*. GB Advisors. http://www.gb-advisors.com/ai-and-crm.
82. Roll, Ido, and Ruth Wylie. "Evolution and Revolution in Artificial Intelligence in Education." *International Journal of Artificial Intelligence in Education*, vol. 26, no. 2, 2016, pp. 582–599., doi:10.1007/s40593-016-0110-3
83. Ruivo, P., Mestre, A., Johansson, B., & Oliveira, T. (2014). Defining the ERP and CRM Integrative Value. *Procedia Technology, 16*, 704–709. https://doi.org/10.1016/j.protcy.2014.10.019
84. Salesforce. *The 6 Biggest Benefits of CRM*. Salesforce.com. https://www.salesforce.com/ap/hub/crm/benefits-of-crm
85. Sandhu, R., Kaur, J., & Thapar, V. (2017). An effective framework for finding similar cases of dengue from audio and text data using domain thesaurus and case base reasoning. *Enterprise Information Systems, 12*(2), 155–172. https://doi.org/10.1080/17517575.2017.1287429
86. Sarwat, M., Levandoski, J. J., Eldawy, A., & Mokbel, M. F. (2014). LARS*: An Efficient and Scalable Location-Aware Recommender System. *IEEE Transactions on Knowledge and Data Engineering, 26*(6), 1384–1399. https://doi.org/10.1109/tkde.2013.29
87. Schlögl, S., Postulka, C., Bernsteiner, R., & Ploder, C. (2019). Artificial Intelligence Tool Penetration in Business: Adoption, Challenges and Fears. *Communications in Computer and Information Science Knowledge Management in Organizations*, 259–270. https://doi.org/10.1007/978-3-030-21451-7_22
88. Shaikhina, T., Lowe, D., Daga, S., Briggs, D., Higgins, R., & Khovanova, N. (2019). Decision tree and random forest models for outcome prediction in antibody incompatible kidney transplantation. *Biomedical Signal Processing and Control, 52*, 456-462. doi:10.1016/j.bspc.2017.01.012

89. Sharma, H., & Kumar, S. (2016). A Survey on Decision Tree Algorithms of Classification in Data Mining. *International Journal of Science and Research (IJSR)*, *5*(4), 2094-2097. doi:10.21275/v5i4.nov162954

90. Singh, A., Rana, A., & Ranjan, J. (2015). Data mining techniques and its effect in customer relationship management. *International Journal of Data Analysis Techniques and Strategies*, *7*(4), 406. https://doi.org/10.1504/ijdats.2015.073862

91. Sohrabi, B., Vanani, I.R., & Shineh, M.B. (2017). Designing a Predictive Analytics Solution for Evaluating the Scientific Trends in Information Systems Domain. *Webology, 14*.

92. Soni, N., Sharma, E. K., Singh, N., & Kapoor, A. (2018). Impact of Artificial Intelligence on Business. In *Digital Innovations, Transformation, and Society Conference* 2018 (Digits 2018). pp (Vol. 10).

93. Soni, N., Sharma, E. K., Singh, N., & Kapoor, A. (2020). Artificial Intelligence in Business: From Research and Innovation to Market Deployment. *Procedia Computer Science*, *167*, 2200–2210. https://doi.org/10.1016/j.procs.2020.03.272

94. Sun, S., Cao, Z., Zhu, H., & Zhao, J. (2020). A Survey of Optimization Methods From a Machine Learning Perspective. *IEEE Transactions on Cybernetics, 50*(8), 3668-3681. doi:10.1109/tcyb.2019.2950779

95. Sun, Z., Han, L., Huang, W., Wang, X., Zeng, X., Wang, M., & Yan, H. (2015). Recommender systems based on social networks. *Journal of Systems and Software*, *99*, 109–119. https://doi.org/10.1016/j.jss.2014.09.019

96. Syam, N., & Sharma, A. (2018). Waiting for a sales renaissance in the fourth industrial revolution: Machine learning and artificial intelligence in sales research and practice. *Industrial Marketing Management*, *69*, 135–146. https://doi.org/10.1016/j.indmarman.2017.12.01

97. Tan, Z., Xu, L., Zhong, W., Guo, X., & Wang, G. (2018). Online activity recognition and daily habit modeling for solitary elderly through indoor position-based stigmergy. *Engineering Applications of Artificial Intelligence*, *76*, 214–225. https://doi.org/10.1016/j.engappai.2018.08.009

98. Tudor, A., Bâra, A., & Botha, I. (2011). Data mining algorithms and techniques research in CRM systems.

99. Ünvan, Y. A. (2020). Market basket analysis with association rules. *Communications in Statistics - Theory and Methods*, 1–14. https://doi.org/10.1080/03610926.2020.1716255

100. Venkatesan, R., Petersen, J. A., & Guissoni, L. (2017). Measuring and Managing Customer Engagement Value Through the Customer Journey. *Customer Engagement Marketing*, 53–74. https://doi.org/10.1007/978-3-319-61985-9_3

101. Vieira, A. (2015). Predicting online user behaviour using deep learning algorithms. *ArXiv, abs/1511.06247*.

102. Vincent, P., Larochelle, H., Bengio, Y., & Manzagol, P.-A. (2008). Extracting and composing robust features with denoising autoencoders. *Proceedings of the 25th International Conference on Machine Learning - ICML '08*. https://doi.org/10.1145/1390156.1390294

103. Wang, Y., Yao, H., & Zhao, S. (2016). Auto-encoder based dimensionality reduction. *Neurocomputing, 184*, 232–242. https://doi.org/10.1016/j.neucom.2015.08.104

104. Wiesner, M., & Pfeifer, D. (2014). Health Recommender Systems: Concepts, Requirements, Technical Basics and Challenges. *International Journal of Environmental Research and Public Health, 11*(3), 2580–2607. https://doi.org/10.3390/ijerph110302580

105. Writer, S. (2020, August 19). *A Brief History of Customer Relationship Management*. CRM Switch. https://crmswitch.com/crm-industry/crm-industry-history/.

106. Xu, A., Liu, Z., Guo, Y., Sinha, V., & Akkiraju, R. (2017). A New Chatbot for Customer Service on Social Media. *Proceedings of the 2017 CHI Conference on Human Factors in Computing Systems*. https://doi.org/10.1145/3025453.3025496

107. Yenala, H., Jhanwar, A., Chinnakotla, M. K., & Goyal, J. (2017). Deep learning for detecting inappropriate content in text. *International Journal of Data Science and Analytics, 6*(4), 273–286. https://doi.org/10.1007/s41060-017-0088-4

108. Zhang, Z. (2018). Improved Adam Optimizer for Deep Neural Networks. *2018 IEEE/ACM 26th International Symposium on Quality of Service (IWQoS)*. https://doi.org/10.1109/iwqos.2018.8624183

109. Zhang, F., & Zhou, Q. (2014). HHT–SVM: An online method for detecting profile injection attacks in collaborative recommender systems. *Knowledge-Based Systems, 65*, 96–105. https://doi.org/10.1016/j.knosys.2014.04.020

110. Zhou, X., Bargshady, G., Abdar, M., Tao, X., Gururajan, R., & Chan, K. (2019). A Case Study of Predicting Banking Customers Behaviour by Using Data Mining. *2019 6th International Conference on Behavioral, Economic and Socio-Cultural Computing (BESC)*. https://doi.org/10.1109/besc48373.2019.8963436

Ingram Content Group UK Ltd.
Milton Keynes UK
UKHW050149080623
422954UK00021B/842